ARCHITECTURE IN ITALY

ARCHITECTURE IN ITALY

a handbook
for travellers
and students

MARTIN S. BRIGGS
F.R.I.B.A.

WITH DRAWINGS BY THE AUTHOR
AND PHOTOGRAPHS

LONDON: J. M. DENT & SONS LTD
NEW YORK: E. P. DUTTON & CO INC

Dedicated to
The British School at Rome

Contents

Illustrations

PLATES

LINE DRAWINGS IN THE TEXT

Greek and Etruscan Settlements in Italy

B, Bologna; F, Florence; G, Genoa; M, Milan; N, Naples;
P, Palermo; R., Rome; T, Turin; V, Venice.

I

Before the Romans

IN DECIDING upon a title for this little book, which is intended for English-speaking visitors to Italy and for students of its architecture, an obvious choice had to be made between *Italian Architecture* and *Architecture in Italy*. There is a subtle difference between the two which needs some explanation and justification at the outset. The former title implies definite characteristics of style, and has been applied or misapplied to certain periods of Italian architecture in various ways by various authorities at various times.

Thus rather more than a century ago—in 1859 to be precise—when the influence of Ruskin was at its height and *The Stones of Venice* had only recently appeared, there was a great controversy in Parliament about the style of the proposed new government offices in Whitehall. One party advocated their design in the Gothic style, then at the summit of its popularity; but Sir William Tite, M.P., who was awarded the Gold Medal of the R.I.B.A. in that very year, demanded that they should be changed to "Italian." As a result of an acrimonious debate Sir Gilbert Scott, R.A., their designer, was compelled to alter the style from "Gothic" to "Italian," by which was meant Italian of the Renaissance period, and

I

so we see them today. According to Hansard's official
report, Tite argued that there could be little doubt that
the Italian style would be more suited to the wants of
common life, and that Gothic would be very incon-
venient; while Lord Palmerston remarked, in a violently
anti-Gothic speech, that it would mean "going back to
the barbarism of the Dark Ages." Eventually Scott had to
sacrifice his own taste and his "conscience," characteris-
tically and smugly recording in his *Recollections* that "to
resign would be to give up a sort of property which Provi-
dence had placed in the hands of my family." What Tite
meant by "Italian architecture" may be seen in his own
design for the church of St James at Gerrards Cross, built
in 1858-9. Its style is unquestionably very un-English and
rather Italian, something between the "Lombard" and
"Early Renaissance" phases of Italian architecture, with
a campanile and a curious dome. Again, when Tite died
in 1873 he left a part of his substantial fortune to establish
the R.I.B.A. "Tite Prize" to be awarded annually "to
promote the study of *Italian* architecture"; and it seems
clear that his intention was to encourage students to con-
centrate on Italian Renaissance architecture, not on the
florid and finicky Gothic of the Doge's Palace and other
Venetian Gothic buildings extolled by his contemporary
Ruskin, who wrote of Italian Renaissance architecture as
a "foul torrent." What Tite's ghost is now thinking of
modern holders of his prize who tend to admire the great
new railway station at Rome and the reinforced-concrete
marvels of Professor Nervi—described in the last chapter
of this book—can only be imagined.

Moreover, a volume dealing with "Italian" architecture should include many of its modern examples outside Italy itself, e.g. in Tripoli and Cyrenaica, now Libya

(occupied by Italy from 1911 to 1943), Ethiopia and Somalia. In all these countries Italian architects showed excellent taste in adapting the traditional native styles to modern requirements; as also in the island of Rhodes, occupied 1912–47. But today the republic of Italy has no colonial possessions, thanks to the Second World War; and our study of her architecture may properly be confined to her present political and geographical boundaries.

It is only at certain periods of history that Italy has been a homogeneous entity. Thus in the remote days of the Emperor Augustus (27 B.C.–A.D. 14) Italy comprised, within its eleven regions, almost exactly the same mainland area as it does today, plus Istria. After the break-up of the Roman Empire at the end of the 5th century it retained its identity as the "Kingdom of Italy" under Odoacer (d. 493); but thereafter it became involved in endless invasions by Goths, Lombards and Byzantines; was split up into a variety of small independent city-states and papal territories all through the Middle Ages, forming a part of the Holy Roman Empire and its successors; and did not emerge as a separate state until the Kingdom of Italy was proclaimed in 1861, Rome becoming its capital ten years later. Hence it is only a century since Italy as we now know it achieved a recognized position among the nations of Europe. (Much the same applies, of course, to Belgium and Greece, both founded in 1830, and to several other countries.)

Geographically, however, there are few anomalies in the natural boundaries of Italy, formed mostly by the sea, but on the north by the Alps. There are some slight discrepancies, such as the Italian-speaking Swiss canton of Ticino, on the southern slopes of the Alps; but the only points where Nature has not drawn a line are on the

Riviera coast near Nice and in the district of Istria. Through much of its history the latter has formed a part of Italy, as has also the Dalmatian coast, where many examples of Italian architecture are still be to seen, to say nothing of the Emperor Diocletian's enormous Late Roman palace at Spalato.

As for the Mediterranean islands, Sicily and Sardinia may safely be reckoned a part of Italy; but Corsica has been French for a long time, and in any case does not contain any notable examples of "Italian" architecture.

Hence although, as will be explained shortly, the architecture of Italy was at one period entirely Greek and cannot always be described as distinctively "Italian," there is no doubt about what is meant by the land of Italy; and we must now consider how its climate, its geology, its natural building materials and above all its position in the centre of the Mediterranean during ancient times have conditioned and influenced its architecture.

The climate of Italy is one of the most delightful in the world, but ranges from extreme winter cold in the mountainous regions of the Alps to semi-tropical heat in many southern districts, with a consequent effect upon the design of dwellings large and small. So one finds houses with low-pitched stone roofs like those of Switzerland in some areas, and others elsewhere with flat roofs resembling those of North Africa and other Mediterranean lands. Many of the mountain ranges are volcanic in origin, some volcanoes being still active; while the craters of others—long extinct—have become lakes, e.g. Albano, Bolsena, Bracciano and Nemi. From these volcanic regions is obtained tufa, a conglomerate stone resembling pumice, much used in ancient Roman buildings; but because it was porous it had to be protected by

a facing of stucco. Another volcanic product was pozzolana (*pulvis puteolanus* in Latin), deriving its name from
Pozzuoli (Lat. Puteoli), near Naples, and also found in the
Alban Hills near Rome. This volcanic earth, when mixed
with lime, forms a very useful fireproof cement; and it
made possible the wonderful achievements of the Romans
in building the great concrete vaults and domes over their
thermae (public baths), described in Chapter 2.

The finest building stone in Italy is travertine (*lapis
tiburtinus* in Latin), so called because it was chiefly
quarried at Tivoli (Lat. Tibur) near Rome. This is a
cream or brown limestone derived from deposits in the
valleys of the Tiber and Anio. It was used in ancient
Roman times for the Colosseum, and for the exterior
walls and colonnades of St Peter's—all in Rome—during
the Renaissance period. Other popular Italian building
stones are and were peperino and Alban stone. The nature
and the use in antiquity of these and of all other building
materials are fully and graphically described by the Roman
architect Vitruvius, whose famous book, *De Architectura*,
was written in the 1st century B.C.

Excellent sandstone is found in Tuscany, and was
largely used in the great Renaissance palaces of Florence.
The Greek temples at Selinus, described on pp. 13–14, were
built of local limestone, but covered with a thin coat of
stucco; and many others in southern Italy and Sicily were
also of stone. Cream-coloured stone from Istria was much
used in Venice.

Marble was not introduced into Italian architecture
until the 1st century B.C., and was rare in the time of
Augustus; but the great quarries of white marble at
Carrara near Pisa were opened soon afterwards. Greek
white marbles from Hymettus and Pentelicus came to be

exported to Italy, together with various coloured marbles; also granites from Egypt, Elba and Naxos; and red basalt, known as porphyry, from Egypt, for great mono-lithic columns as well as for the geometrical paving known as *opus Alexandrinum* (p. 32). It was the Emperor Augustus who found Rome "a city of brick" and left it "a city of marble," using for the purpose white Carrara marble, then known as *marmor Lunense*.

The Verona district produced red and orange marbles, much used in Venice, where Istrian marble was also popular; and from the neighbourhood of Siena came both white and yellow marbles, the latter called *giallo di Siena*. The Romans also opened quarries on the north coast of Africa for *giallo antico* or Numidian (yellow) marble. Other African marbles were grey cipollino, rosso and alabaster. The marble for the medieval façades of Pisa and Orvieto cathedrals (Chapters 4–5) was obtained from ruined Roman buildings in Rome and Ostia. The marble shafts in the Early Christian basilican churches of Rome and Ravenna (Chapter 3) were largely rifled from older Roman buildings.

The internal (and sometimes external) marble facings of many Italian medieval churches came from the same sources, as did their marble pavements and mosaics. The small cubes (tesserae) consisting of marble and other ornamental stones used for mosaic work in Italy from very early times were often made from imported material. This interesting craft is described fully by Vitruvius (vii. 1), and was practised widely in Italy from his date onwards for many centuries, notably in the work of the Cosmati family (pp. 48, etc.) in the 13th century. Examples from Rome, Ravenna, Venice, etc., are cited in later chapters in this book.

Bricks were extensively used in Italy from the earliest times, but up to the age of Augustus and Vitruvius seem to have been of sun-dried clay. After that date kiln-burnt bricks came into general use. Vitruvius deals fully with brick-earth and its preparation, and evidently it was obtainable without difficulty. Suitable clay for making roofing tiles was also available.

As for timber, Italy is fairly well wooded in parts, and cypress, ilex and stone-pine appear to be indigenous; while forests of oak, chestnut, larch, and fir are not uncommon. There is a famous pinewood (the *Pineta*) at Ravenna and another near Ostia. From the invaluable Vitruvius we gather that he was familiar with the properties and practical uses of oak, elm, poplar, cypress, fir, pine, larch, cedar, etc. Only in the case of cedar does he suggest that it was imported (from Crete, Syria and Africa), while he states that larch is known only "on the banks of the River Po and the shores of the Adriatic"; on the other hand he speaks of "Turkey oak" (*Quercus cerris*), which may or may not have been imported into Italy. At any rate we may say that Italy possesses a certain amount of home-grown timber suitable for building purposes.

It remains now to consider the geographical position of Italy, lying athwart the Mediterranean half-way or thereabouts between Gibraltar at one end and Constantinople, Egypt and Jerusalem at the other; and the effects of that position upon its architecture.

Waves of invaders from all directions—north, south, east and west—have tramped and trampled over Italy for three thousand years at least; and though the earliest buildings that merit the name of architecture are no older than *c.* 600 B.C., mention must now be made of earlier migrations in order to provide a background to my story.

B

In the Old Stone Age there was no Mediterranean Sea, only two lakes between Europe and Africa, separated from each other by a "land-bridge" from Tunis in Africa to Sicily and Calabria in Italy; and another "land-bridge" at Gibraltar united Morocco with Spain. In the Neolithic or New Stone Age which followed, the Mediterranean had become a sea, and the land-bridges had gone; but otherwise the main geographical features existed as they are today; and Neolithic men, living in artificially constructed dwellings, may be regarded as the aboriginal inhabitants of Italy. They were members of the so-called "Mediterranean race" and entered the country from two directions. One group crossed from Africa at the Straits of Gibraltar, and then traversed Iberia (Spain) and southern France, entering Italy on the Ligurian coast, hence their name of "Ibero-Ligurians." The other stream, also coming from Africa, started near Tunis and reached Calabria, "island-hopping" via Sicily and some smaller islands. These were the "Siculans." From these two sources the majority of South Italians are descended. At first, c. 2500 B.C., they lived in caves; but in some districts they constructed huts of "wattle-and-daub," known to us from models in pottery found in Rome, the Alban Hills and Tuscany, and today exhibited in many Italian museums. These huts were circular or oval in plan, and were roofed with rough-hewn timber beams. Generally the earth floors were sunk two or three feet below ground level, and there was a central hearth of clay.

Early in the Bronze Age, just before 2000 B.C., another stream of invaders arrived, this time from the north, and apparently from Switzerland. They built their dwellings on piles in shallow water for defensive purposes. They settled in the Italian Lakes area and near modern Venice.

Three centuries or so later, *c.* 1700 B.C., came much more important invaders from the highly civilized Danube basin, who also favoured pile dwellings, but on dry land, known as *Terremare*. These people are sometimes called "Proto-Italici," and are regarded as the ancestors of the Latins or Romans. They kept in touch with their Danubian homeland, so that northern Italy, about the 13th century B.C., began to benefit from European commerce.

Yet another stream, known today as the "Villanovans," entered Italy from the north-east, via Istria and the Tyrolean passes, occupying the east coast as far south as Rimini, the west coast from the Arno to the Tiber (on the future site of Rome), and all the interior of Italy between those limits. The name of Villanovans has been given to them because of their ancient cemetery at Villanova near Bologna. Their period extends into the Iron Age, during which the famous race of Etruscans arrived from Asia Minor in the 9th century. They are of importance in architectural history, as distinct from archaeology, because in later years they did erect buildings which have some claim to be regarded as architecture, before the Romans appear in our story. None of these buildings, however, can be dated earlier than the 6th century B.C., or thereabouts, and a description of their ruins may be deferred to a later stage (p. 15); for by that time the first Greek settlements had been founded in Italy and Sicily. These are of supreme significance in the history of architecture in Italy.

When they began, in the 8th century B.C., Greece was not a single country but a land contested between a number of small rival states. Seeking a peaceful life with opportunities for trade, many Greeks crossed the straits to Italy in search of new homes. Sailing from Euboea one group founded Cumae near Naples *c.* 760 B.C., afterwards settling also at Naples. Bands of Dorians from Corinth seized Syracuse in Sicily from earlier settlers in 733; Laconians entered Tarentum in 705. Peloponnesians founded Sybaris and Croton *c.* 720–710, followed by Metapontum and Posidonia (Paestum, or "Pesto" in Italian)—all these on the mainland. Selinus (Selinunte), Agrigentum, and Gela (all these in Sicily) were founded later.

The Greek buildings surviving in southern Italy and Sicily are almost all temples, and are all in ruins. With the exception of one temple at Locri in Calabria, and un-roofed theatres at Syracuse and Pompeii, they are all temples of the Doric Order. They are situated at Syracuse, Selinus, Agrigentum (Agrigento in Italian) and Segesta in Sicily; at Tarentum, Paestum, Pompeii, Metapontum and Locri on the Italian mainland. They range in date from *c.* 575 B.C. to *c.* 250 B.C. The Doric Order is the oldest, sturdiest and simplest of the "orders" of columns (first defined by Vitruvius in the Augustan Age and since adopted as a standard by all architects throughout the Western world; see p. 19).

The Doric Order, used in these very early temples, did not attain its full maturity and refinement until the famous Parthenon was built at Athens in 447–432 B.C.; and the examples in Sicily and southern Italy are comparatively clumsy and crude in design. Moreover, unlike the Parthenon, which is of marble, they are of limestone or sandstone. In some of them, at any rate, the columns were coated with stucco. The Doric Order was so called after the Dorian Greeks who spoke the Doric tongue, and probably arrived in the Peloponnesus (southern Greece) from Crete and the north *c.* 1100 B.C. In the Greek

Doric Order of architecture (p. 19, A) the fluted columns have no bases, and have cushion-shaped capitals supporting a flat block (the abacus) upon which rest the beams of the superstructure (the entablature). This type of column, and its beams, are supposed to have been derived and imitated from earlier timber prototypes. The tapered

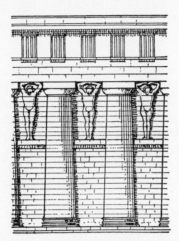

Atlantes at the Greek Doric temple
of Zeus Olympius, Agrigentum
(c. 470 B.C.)

columns are very sturdy, their lower diameter being from a quarter to a sixth of their height, are rather closely spaced, and are usually built up of horizontal sections ("drums"), because a whole column of this size could not have been obtained from a monolith—a single stone.

Of the Doric temples on the mainland already mentioned, those at Tarentum (Taranto in Italian), Locri and

Pompeii are now represented only by mere fragments or foundations and so are hardly worth a visit. At Paestum, close to the sea near Salerno and 48 miles from Naples on the main railway line to Reggio, are three Doric temples in a walled enclosure. The largest and latest—the so-called "Temple of Poseidon" or Neptune (c. 460 B.C.)—is one of the finest examples in Italy, with all its thirty-six outer columns still standing, as well as some of the smaller inner columns. The outer columns are of impressive size, 29 feet high and 6 feet 11 inches in diameter at the base. (The reader should pause to consider how colossal these dimensions are.) These columns are of travertine stone coated with stucco. The massive internal walls of the sanctuary or temple proper also survive. The outer measurements of this fine building are approximately 200 feet by 80 feet.

The adjoining so-called "Basilica," a temple also apparently dedicated to Poseidon, is much earlier (c. 565 B.C.) and is nearly as large. Its fifty columns are of travertine stone. The third of the trio, the Temple of Ceres or Demeter (c. 530 B.C.), is much smaller and is of limestone and sandstone.

Of the two Doric temples at Metapontum (Metaponto in Italian), which is on the railway and near the sea between Naples and Taranto, the more important is the building (c. 520 B.C.) known as the Tavole Paladine ("tables or seats of the Paladins," i.e. Saracen chiefs). Fifteen crumbling columns are still standing, but the general effect, in a lonely situation, is depressing. The other temple at Metapontum is known locally as the Chiesa di Sansone ("Samson's Church"), and has stone columns cased with stucco. All these temples at Paestum and Metapontum are ruined; but they escaped further damage in the Second World War, as did those in Sicily now to be described.

There are remains of three Doric temples at Syracuse, on the east coast of the island. One of these is the ruined former Temple of Athena or Minerva (*c.* 470 B.C. or later) the massive columns of which are now surprisingly incorporated in the walls of the Baroque cathedral or Duomo (p. 146). These columns are of almost exactly the same size as those in the Temple of Poseidon at Paestum (p. 12). In its former glory this temple had doors of gold and ivory, and the statue of Athena standing on the pediment, with a golden shield, was visible from far out at sea.

Much older and much larger was the ruined Doric Temple of Zeus Olympius at Syracuse (*c.* 575 B.C.), but only two stumps of its enormous columns now survive. The third example,

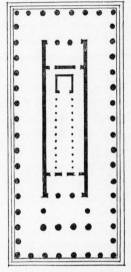

Great Temple at Selinus (pseudipteral octastyle)

the Temple of Apollo, is slightly smaller, with six columns at each end and nineteen on each flank.

Another important group of early Doric temples in Sicily is at Selinus (Selinunte in Italian), on a walled promontory or acropolis near the western end of the island. They number at least seven and are referred to in guidebooks and textbooks by distinctive letters of the alphabet. In date they range from *c.* 540 to *c.* 490 B.C. The oldest of them, the Temple of Apollo, measures approximately 361 by 164 feet, and is thus one of the largest Greek temples known. Its colossal size is slightly surpassed, however, by the Temple of Zeus Olympius, sometimes called the Olympieum (c. 470 B.C.), at Akragas or Agrigentum on the south coast of Sicily. Of these Greek temples in Sicily and South Italy—as in Greece itself—it may be remarked that, although their ancestry may be traced ultimately to timber construction, they were built entirely of stone or marble, without any use of timber except for the rafters of the sloping roofs, all of which have perished long ago. Apart from temples, the only notable Greek building of which remains exist in South Italy and Sicily is the unroofed theatre at Syracuse, c. 400 B.C.

Before turning to the later "Hellenistic" (i.e. late Greek or Greco-Roman) architecture of Pompeii it is necessary to consider the adventures of the Etruscans, who, as already mentioned (p. 9), arrived in Italy some time before 800 B.C., probably from Lydia in Asia Minor. They gave their name to Etruria, the district around the River Arno, and eventually (7th century B.C.) formed a famous confederation of twelve cities including some of the following: Veii (near Rome), Tarquinii (near Corneto, now known as Corneto Tarquinia), Clusium (Chiusi), Caere (Cerveteri), Cortona, Vetulonia or Volaterrae (Volterra), Vulci or Vulcia, Volsinii or Velsina (Orvieto), Perusia (Perugia), Arretium (Arezzo), Falerii (Città Castellana). This group was called "Etruria Propria," and north of it was formed "Etruria Circumpadana" in the Po valley, another confederation of twelve cities, with Felsina (Bologna) at its head. At one period there was also a third group in the neighbourhood of Rome-Naples, but this was obliterated by Syracusans from Sicily in a battle at Cumae in 474 B.C., and Etruria Propria was defeated by the Romans at Veii in 396 B.C. Thus any architectural remains of the Etruscans must be dated between 800 and 400 B.C., and in fact they are very scanty. There was a time not long ago when the ancient main sewer of Rome, the Cloaca Maxima, was acclaimed as a relic of Etruscan architecture and also as a very early example of an arch; but both theories are rejected by modern scholars, and certainly it is not a true arch.

What little is definitely known of Etruscan architecture can be summarized under four heads: temples, dwelling-houses, tombs and arched gateways. Any visitor to Italy, however unacademic, can hardly fail to enjoy a visit to the admirably arranged Etruscan galleries at the Villa di Papa Giulio, in itself a beautiful building by Vignola (p. 111); and there he will find a convincing full-size model or reconstruction of the Etruscan temple at Alatri (3rd century B.C.), about 50 miles south-east of Rome. This has a single *cella* (sanctuary) and a portico with two rather clumsy Doric columns at either end. The low sloping roof has a richly moulded pediment (gable) at either end, the ornamental details being in terra-cotta. Some scholars regard it as an incorrect restoration; but at least it does give us some idea of what an Etruscan temple must have looked like—not exactly Greek and not exactly Roman. There are ruined and fragmentary examples elsewhere: at Staricum (Conca), Falerii (Città Castellana), Marzabotto (near Bologna), etc.

The nature of Etruscan dwelling-houses is to be inferred from their representation in tombs carved out of solid rock, especially in the famous necropolis or cemetery at Cerveteri, which lies about 25 miles north-west of Rome. In these tombs the rafters of the sloping roof are realistically carved in the solid stone ceilings. Other interesting relics of Etruscan architecture and sculpture may be seen at the Vatican Museum and in the Etruscan Museum at Florence.

The most important question about Etruscan architecture, still unsolved, is whether the Romans derived the arch, the most distinctive feature of their buildings, from the Etruscans or from elsewhere. It is certain that they did not invent the arch—that was done centuries earlier in the orient—but they did use it very effectively in or about the 3rd century B.C., e.g. in two arched gateways at Perugia and in some gateways of their other cities. The latest pronouncement on this topic is given, confidently and categorically, by Dr H. Plommer in his *Ancient and Classical Architecture* (1956), p. 223: "Whoever taught the Romans the use of the arch, it was not the Etruscans."

In the excavated ruins of Pompeii there are the remains of a Greek Doric temple of *c.* 550 B.C. which was buried, like everything else in the town, by the terrible eruption of Vesuvius in A.D. 79. A few years earlier, in A.D. 63, a fearful earthquake had destroyed the greater part of its buildings; and between that date and A.D. 79 a large number of them had been rebuilt. It therefore provides a unique example of a Greco-Roman or "Hellenistic" town of the 1st century. It had become a favourite resort of wealthy citizens, even of some Roman emperors, before the final calamity; and it is well laid out in the form of an ellipse, divided into rectangular plots. The streets vary in width from 14 to 24 feet and are paved with rectangular blocks of lava. At the principal intersections there were fountains. Whole streets of shops, with their counters and other fittings, have been pre-served. There were two spacious *fora* surrounded by colonnades. Public buildings included two bathing establishments, a basilica, a large store, open and covered theatres. The numerous houses were of all sizes and types, usually planned round an inner courtyard and containing lavishly decorated rooms. The tragic event which buried them in A.D. 79 has preserved them in all their beauty for posterity, and no visitor to Italy should neglect an opportunity of seeing Pompeii, easily accessible from Naples.

2

Roman Architecture

from *c.* 10 B.C. to *c.* A.D. 330

As EVERY schoolboy knows or should know, Rome is said to have been founded by one Romulus in 753 B.C. Yet scholars who have compiled chronologies record hardly any buildings of importance before 100 B.C. The chief exceptions—neither of which can be called exactly architecture—are the Milvian Bridge (Ital. Ponte Molle or Ponte Milvio), still standing but restored, and an aqueduct, the Acqua Marcia, 144 B.C.

During the next seventy years, up to the accession of the Emperor Augustus (31 B.C.), modern historians mention temples at Tivoli and Cori (two each), Palestrina (Praeneste) and Assisi; the Temple of Fortuna Virilis, the Tullianum or Mamertine Prison, the Tabularium, the Regium and the Basilica—all in Rome; and the roofed theatre at Aosta. It is a meagre output for the Roman Empire in half a century! When Augustus boasted that he had found Rome "a city of brick" (presumably mud-brick) and left it "a city of marble," he evidently meant that he had made a clean sweep of much of the preceding architecture, such as it was; and indeed most of the great

18

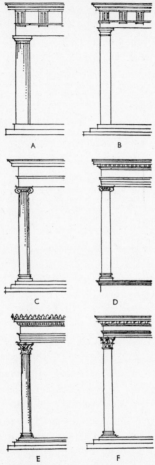

Orders: The classical (Greek and Roman) orders of Architecture
A, Greek Doric; B, Roman Doric; C, Greek Ionic;
D, Roman Ionic; E, Greek Corinthian;
F, Roman Corinthian.

examples of Roman architecture date from long after his
time. It was only then that Rome itself became a really
fine city, with its palaces, triumphal arches, stadia, theatres
and amphitheatres, temples, tombs, thermae, basilicas;
and it was later still that comparable Roman architecture
began to blossom elsewhere in Italy.

Capitals: A, Roman Doric; B, Roman Ionic;
C, Roman Corinthian; D, Byzantine.

For much of what we know about Roman architecture
and building methods in the days of Augustus we have to
rely upon the manual *De Architectura*, compiled by the
architect Vitruvius (1st century B.C.), already mentioned.
In that work he also attempts to trace the origin of contemporary Roman architecture to that of ancient Greece,
which he had evidently studied to some effect. He had a
very tidy mind; and when he had devised his system of
classifying Greek and Roman buildings according to the

"orders" of their columns—"Doric," "Ionic" and "Corinthian" in both cases—he found that the remains of Etruscan temples fell rather outside his scheme; so he added the "Tuscan Order" of columns and of temples, the columns being very simple and sturdy, their height seven times their lower diameter. In cold fact, however, this order was a product of his own brain, and may be ignored by modern visitors to Italy. (There is a fairly recent example of its revived use in the portico of St Paul's Church, Covent Garden, London.)

There are few examples of the Ionic Order in Italy, the Corinthian Order being the most popular. Both these orders were derived from Greece, as their names imply: the former, with its spiral capitals, from Ionia in Asia Minor; the latter, with its bell-shaped capital wreathed in acanthus leaves, from Corinth. Roman taste tended to be more exuberant and florid than Greek, hence the Corinthian Order was generally favoured. The following is a short list of examples of temples of the two types.

IONIC

Tivoli.	The Rectangular Temple	c. 80 B.C.
Rome.	Temple of Fortuna Virilis	c. 40 B.C.

CORINTHIAN

Tivoli.	The Circular Temple	c. 80 B.C.
Praeneste.	Temple of Fortune	c. 80 B.C.
Assisi.	Temple of Minerva	? c. 40 B.C.
Rome.	Circular Temple of Vesta by the Tiber	? c. 31 B.C.
,,	Temple of Divus Julius	c. 40–29 B.C.
,,	,, ,, Concord	7 B.C.–A.D. 10
,,	,, ,, Mars Ultor	2 B.C.
Pompeii.	,, ,, Fortuna Augusta	before A.D. 3

Rome.			Temple of Castor	A.D. 6
„		„ „	Vespasian	A.D. 80
„		The Pantheon (circular)		c. A.D. 120
„		Temple of Venus and Rome (rebuilt c. 310)		
				A.D. 135
„	„	„	Divus Hadrianus	c. A.D. 140
„	„	„	Serapis	c. A.D. 170
„	„	„	Minerva Medica (or Nymphaeum)	
				c. A.D. 260
„	„	„	Romulus (circular)	c. A.D. 307–315
„	„	„	Saturn	c. A.D. 320

It will be noticed that in this long list four circular temples are mentioned. Of these, the Pantheon demands separate treatment, for it differs from all the others and is of outstanding importance in the history of architecture. Nothing quite like it had ever been erected before. Dedicated "to all the gods" (Gk *pan*, all; *theos*, a god), it consists of a huge domed structure with a portico of columns of the Corinthian Order. The former was certainly erected by the emperor in A.D. 120–4. The date of the latter is still disputed among scholars, some of whom regard it as coeval with the rotunda; others as a part of an earlier building by Agrippa incorporated as a frontispiece by Hadrian in the new Pantheon, as the inscription over the portico implies; others again ascribing it to a date later than Hadrian, possibly the reign of Septimius Severus. Externally the Pantheon has been unkindly compared to a gasometer, which indeed it does resemble in size and shape; but one must remember that it was formerly faced with marble, and its dome covered with gilded tiles. Internally it is one of the wonders of the world. It consists of an enormous brick drum with walls about 20 feet thick (but pierced with recesses), and having

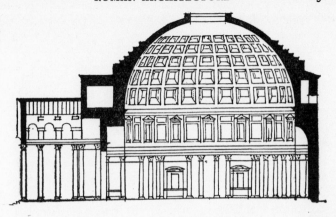

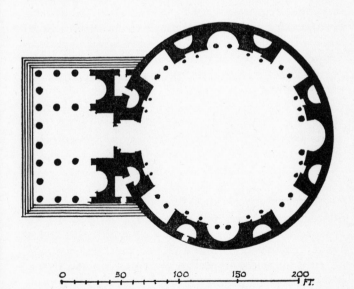

The Pantheon, Rome: Plan and Section

C

an internal diameter of 142 feet 6 inches. At a height of
about 70 feet above the floor an approximately hemispherical dome rises to a so-called "eye," an orifice 27
feet in diameter, open to the sky, which supplies the only
source of light to the immense interior of the building.
The effect is magnificent. The construction of the dome is
a *tour de force*, its colossal weight being reduced by a series
of coffers or recesses over its surface, between the ribs.
The Pantheon is almost the only great building of ancient
Rome that is in perfect condition internally today. In
A.D. 609 Pope Boniface II consecrated the building as a
Christian church, "S. Maria Rotonda."

Bronze was largely used in the Pantheon for both
structural and decorative purposes. The magnificent
bronze doors still exist,[1] together with some other
features; but much fine bronze work has been removed.
The gilt bronze roof tiles, already mentioned, were
stripped off in 663 by the Emperor Constans II, and were
being transferred by him to Constantinople when they
were captured near Syracuse by the Saracens. Lead roofing was substituted by Gregory III in 735. As an inscription on the left of the entrance to the Pantheon states,
Urban VIII in 1632 had the bronze roof-trusses of the
portico melted down, thus producing 200 tons of metal.
This was utilized partly for cannon (*bellica tormenta*) for
the Castle of S. Angelo, and partly for Bernini's great
baldacchino over the high altar of St Peter's (p. 125). As
the Goths had previously rifled the Pantheon of other
bronze features, this action by Urban VIII (a Barberini
pope) provoked an ironical epigram from Pasquino:
"Quod non fecerunt barbari, fecerunt Barberini."

[1] Illustrated on Fig. 383 in my Chapter XII in *A History of Tech-
nology*, vol. ii (Oxford, 1957).

It has been suggested that Hadrian, a layman, could not possibly have designed this masterpiece himself, and must have employed a professional architect; but although many famous patrons of architecture (e.g. William of Wykeham in England) have been credited with designs made for them by trained architects, it does seem that Hadrian, who is known to have been well versed in several arts and sciences, may actually have created the Pantheon. The great Italian scholar Rivoira, in his book on *Roman Architecture* (1919), accepts the fact and also attributes to Hadrian the invention of "a skeleton framework in vaults of circular form." Whatever may be the truth, it is certain that Hadrian's numerous ventures into architecture aroused the jealousy of Apollodorus of Damascus (c. A.D. 60–c. A.D. 130), a professional architect who had several sharp encounters with his imperial patron and employer. On one occasion Apollodorus snubbed Hadrian, then a young man, in the presence of the then emperor, Trajan, his guardian, telling Hadrian to drop architectural design and turn to painting pumpkins. Soon afterwards Hadrian, apparently swallowing this insult, showed Apollodorus another design, for a new temple in Rome. The tactless older man remarked that if the deities whose seated statues were in the temple were to stand up they would bump their heads. The result of this second and more serious indiscretion was that Apollodorus himself was first banished and then beheaded by Hadrian, c. A.D. 130. "Those were the days."

With the exception of the Pantheon, which resembled nothing in earlier Greek architecture, the design of Roman temples was clearly based on that architecture; and the same ancestry can be traced in the design of Roman theatres. These were erected all over the Empire;

and there is an excellent specimen in England, *c.* A.D. 140–50, at Verulamium near St Albans, where the general arrangements of the stage, orchestra and auditorium can be traced.

In Italy itself the chief surviving example is the Theatre of Marcellus, Rome, 11 B.C., but there are a few fragments of others, e.g. at Fiesole, near Florence, 1st century B.C. As for amphitheatres, the splendid example at Verona was built under Diocletian, *c.* A.D. 290; and there are others at Capua, Pompeii and Pozzuoli in southern Italy; at Syracuse in Sicily; and at Pola in Istria. But of course the most famous Roman amphitheatre in the world is the Flavian Amphitheatre at Rome (*c.* A.D. 75–82), commonly called the Colosseum, on the site of a former lake. Elliptical in plan, it measures about 620 by 500 feet externally, with an elliptical arena about 290 by 180 feet. (*Arena* in Latin means "sand," with which the floor had to be spread at frequent intervals for obvious and rather gruesome reasons.) The outer walls reach the tremendous height of about 160 feet above ground level. The huge audience was protected from the glare of the sun by a great awning, the *velarium*, slung from poles by sailors. Entrance to and exit from the rows of marble seats was provided by *vomitoria* (passages and aisles); and beneath the vast extent of seating were cellars for gladiators and dens for wild beasts. The accommodation for spectators is estimated at about 50,000 persons. No description is called for here of the splendid but often brutal displays that took place in this famous and infamous building; but architecturally it is important as an example of the wholly superfluous use of the various orders in four successive tiers on the exterior: Doric at the bottom, then Ionic, Corinthian and

"Composite" (a hybrid of Corinthian and Ionic) on the upper stages.

Roman stadia (or "circuses") are of less significance architecturally, however impressive their size. They were designed primarily for chariot-races. The Circus Maximus in Rome, which within recent memory was occupied by a hideous gas-works—now removed—provided a track about 2,000 feet long. The site of another, the Circus of Domitian, also in Rome, is now represented by the beautiful Piazza Navona, decorated with Bernini's fountains (p. 125). These Roman facilities for sport and display have been augmented on the grand scale during the present century, as part of Mussolini's campaign for restoring Rome to its ancient status as the capital of the civilized world (see Chapters 13 and 14).

Another feature of Imperial Rome is to be found in the triumphal arches erected in Italy and in other provinces of the Empire. They generally assumed one of two forms: either a single arch or a wide central arch for vehicles flanked on either side by a smaller arch for pedestrians. The heavy superstructure provided a field for bold carvings representing military victories or other events considered worthy of commemoration. In Italy the principal examples are the Arch of Augustus at Rimini, 27 B.C., its namesakes at Aosta, c. 23 B.C., and at Susa, c. 8 B.C., the Arch of Titus at Rome, c. 82 B.C., of Trajan at Benevento, A.D. 114–17, of Septimius Severus, A.D. 203, and of Constantine, A.D. 315—both at Rome. Another type of monumental architecture is seen in Trajan's Column at Rome, A.D. 112, decorated spirally with sculptures in low relief depicting Trajan's victories. At Brindisi are two tall columns marking the southern terminus of the Via Appia or "Appian Way."

The most grandiose and magnificent public buildings erected during the imperial period in Rome are the huge thermae, found especially in Rome itself. They include the thermae of Agrippa, 25–12 B.C.; of Nero, A.D. 62; of Titus, c. A.D. 80; of Trajan, c. A.D. 115; of Caracalla, c. A.D. 215; and of Diocletian, A.D. 306. Only ruined portions remain of the first four; the Baths of Caracalla are also ruined, but are impressive because of their huge size; while the internal splendour of the *calidarium* (= hot bath) of the Baths of Diocletian has been preserved by its skilful transformation under Michelangelo (p. 110) into the church of S. Maria degli Angeli.

These great thermae were much more than mere public baths. The provision for actual bathing was varied and elaborate; but the additional amenities provided—recreational, social, even cultural—corresponded roughly to those of a modern social club. The baths proper occupied a large vaulted building, with the heating-plant beneath it. They usually included a *tepidarium* (warm bath), *calidarium* (hot room with hot bath), *sudatorium* (sweating-room—the hottest room), *frigidarium* (cooling-room), *unctoria* (anointing-rooms), *piscina* (swimming-bath) and *apodyteria* (dressing-rooms). All these—as well as rooms for indoor games, colonnades, shops, lecture-rooms and libraries—were grouped around the xystus, an open space laid out partly as a garden and partly as playing-fields. In England there are remains of small thermae at Wroxeter and at Bath.

One other example of monumental architecture in Rome deserves special mention; the beautiful Ara Pacis (= Altar of Peace), 13–9 B.C., sculptured in marble. It was reconstructed in 1938 from fragments scattered in various museums and elsewhere.

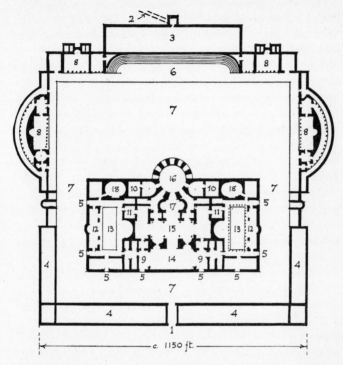

Thermae: Plan of the Baths of Caracalla, Rome (A.D. 211 onwards).
1, Entrance to enclosure; 2, Aqueduct (Acqua Marcia); 3, Reservoirs
(two storeys); 4, Porticus and small chambers; 5, Entrances to central
block of baths etc.; 6, Stadium; 7, Xystus (open space planted with
avenues of trees); 8, Lecture-halls and Libraries; 9, Ante-rooms; 10,
Warm Baths; 11, Hot Baths; 12, Ephebia; 13, Open Peristyle; 14,
Frigidarium; 15, Tepidarium (or possibly the Apodyterium or
"changing-room"; 16, Calidarium; 17, Ante-room or secondary
Tepidarium; 18, Rooms for games.

The type of Roman building which led to "Roman-esque" and then to Gothic church architecture is the basilica. Derived from the Greek word *basileus* (king), the term basilica originally signified a building erected for royal purposes: hence a public hall for the administration of justice and the transaction of business in a Roman city, usually adjoining the forum or market-place. (Later the word came to mean an early Christian church, somewhat resembling a secular basilica in its general plan and arrangements.) The chief Roman secular basilicas were built in Rome itself, and provided shelter from rain and freedom from disturbance—essential conditions for the orderly conduct of legal and commercial business.

The oldest recorded example, the Porcian Basilica, was erected in 184 B.C., and may have been inspired by the Stoa at Athens. It no longer survives, and the oldest remaining example is at Pompeii (*c.* 100 B.C.). In Rome the Basilica Aemilia (*c.* 54–34 B.C.) was followed by the Basilica Julia (31 B.C.–A.D. 14), and the Basilica Ulpia (A.D. 112). The Basilica Nova, begun by Maxentius, was finished by Constantine after A.D. 313. There were basilicas in all the chief cities of the Roman Empire, London among them. The typical Roman basilica, excluding the latest examples, consisted of a long and wide space or "nave," flanked on either side by aisles, which were separated from the nave by a range of columns. Above the aisles were often galleries with flat roofs, and above them again were ranges of windows lighting the nave. The normal Roman secular basilica had no apse, but there was a throne for the judge at the end facing the entrance.

The Basilica Nova of Maxentius, just mentioned, differed from the earlier examples in having a huge brick barrel-vault over the central nave, which is 83 feet wide. This heavy vault naturally exerted a great thrust (i.e. a downward and outward pressure) upon its supporting walls, so the points of support were strengthened by buttresses arched over the flanking aisles. That is why the Roman secular basilica came to be so important in the subsequent general history of architectural development; for not only was its plan and general arrangement the embryo of the later Romanesque and Gothic cathedrals, but its vaulting (adopted partly in order to provide a fireproof roof) was the ancestor of those same great buildings.

The secular basilicas of Rome were placed adjoining the various *fora*. It must be remembered that the Forum Romanum, the oldest of them, was only one of several, e.g. the Forum of Trajan. A forum was provided in every Roman town of any size (e.g. London, Verulamium, etc., in England), and was a central public space for organized or casual gatherings, surrounded by public buildings and colonnades.

Another type of structure, "engineering" rather than architecture, was the arched aqueduct conveying water from a distant source to a city. The most dramatic Roman examples surviving are outside Italy, viz. the Pont du Gard, across a river valley near Nîmes in southern France (? 1st century A.D., 160 feet high); those at Segovia (102 feet) and at Tarragona (83 feet) in Spain; and the largest of all (200 feet), at Antioch in Syria.

All round the city of Rome, however, a modern visitor is impressed by the long lines of broken arches converging upon it from every side, bringing water to the capital from the Alban Hills, across the flat country of the Campagna. At the height of ancient Rome's prosperity, *c.* A.D. 100, they numbered nine in all, and one of them was 60 miles in length.

Much interesting information about the water supply of Imperial Rome, as well as about the actual construction of the aqueducts, is contained in a book *De Aquis* (*c.* A.D. 100), written by one Frontinus, a municipal water-engineer. The actual channel for the water was of rectangular section lined with cement (as can still be seen on

Opus Alexandrinum from church of S. Prassede, Rome
(13th century)

the Pont du Gard). The supporting arches are of stone, chiefly volcanic tufa (cf. p. 4). One of the oldest surviving aqueducts is the Acqua Marcia, about 6 miles long, which has arches of about 18 feet span.

In the city, at the receiving end, the water was distributed by a most elaborate arrangement of cisterns and pipes; and the Roman architect Vitruvius, in his manual *De Architectura*, already quoted, adds something to the accurate description furnished by Frontinus. Both earthenware and lead pipes were used, the former being much cheaper; but Vitruvius prefers them on other grounds, writing that water from them "is much more wholesome than that which is conducted through lead pipes, because lead is found to be harmful to the human system. . . . This we can exemplify from plumbers, since in them the natural colour of the body is replaced by a deep pallor" (VIII. vi. 10).

The amount of water required for the public thermae was of course enormous, in addition to normal domestic needs. The Romans excelled in the internal heating of buildings.

The construction of bridges, like that of aqueducts, is commonly regarded as engineering rather than architecture; and here it is sufficient to mention a few examples in Italy surviving from Roman days: the Pons Milvius (Ital. Ponte Milvio or Ponte Molle), 109 B.C., and the Pons Fabricius (62 B.C.), both in Rome, across the Tiber, and both having arches of very wide span. There is another, between Ivrea and Aosta in northern Italy, with the enormous span of 117 feet.

In Italy, as in England, very few examples survive of Roman dwelling-houses; and one may learn much about their planning without going further afield than Verulamium or Silchester, to say nothing of several fine Roman villas that are still represented by ruined but intelligible fragments in England. Rome can still show some remains of the magnificent palaces of the Caesars on the Palatine, one of the "seven hills of Rome." The Latin word *palatium* is probably derived from the goddess of shepherds, Pales; and in its turn has given us "palace" in English. The Palatine Hill (Mons Palatinus in Latin) formed the very heart of ancient Rome; and Augustus set the fashion by building the Domus Augustiana or Flavia there, to be followed by a succession of

44061

emperors. Among the elaborate complex of buildings the Domus Tiberiana and the Domus Liviae (Ital. Casa di Livia) are the most important. The famous and notorious Domus Aurea (Golden House) of Nero, A.D. 64–9, was altered by his successors, of whom Septimius Severus built the so-called Septizonium early in the 3rd century A.D. The Domus Liviae contains interesting wall-paintings.

Fire, war, decay and changing fashion have caused the disappearance of the dwellings of the Roman populace. At the height of its ancient glory the population of the city was probably between $1\frac{1}{4}$ and $1\frac{1}{2}$ million, as compared with nearly 2 million today. The centre, around the Capitol and the Forum Romanum, was occupied by public buildings and laid out with much splendour and dignity; but between this area and the perimeter of the city walls (to be described hereafter) most of the people lived in tall "flats" or apartments, the bulk of which were erected by speculative builders and private financiers, many of them dishonest.

The ground floor of each block usually consisted of shops (*tabernae*) which had hinged flaps or shutters that could be let down to form a counter projecting over the sidewalk or pavement. The upper storeys were of flimsy timber framing, at first faced with wattle-and-daub, later with concrete. The roofs were covered with wood shingles, later with tiles. Fires and collapses were frequent and often fatal. In the reign of Augustus (27 B.C.–A.D. 14) new building regulations prescribed the use of solid brickwork for the lower part of such buildings, and limited their total height to 70 feet. Still more stringent regulations in the reign of Nero (A.D. 54–68) insisted upon fireproof materials for all external walls. Under Trajan

PLATE I

Rome: Etruscan temple from Alatri, restored (*Photo: Brogi*)

PLATE II

Paestum (Pesto): Temple of Ceres (*Photo: Anderson*)

Pompeii: The House of the Vettii (*Photo: Alinari*)

(A.D. 98–118) the maximum total height was reduced to 60 feet.

These tenements had no provision for sanitation, washing, cooking or heating; but Rome, as we have seen, had a superb and most elaborate system of water supply.

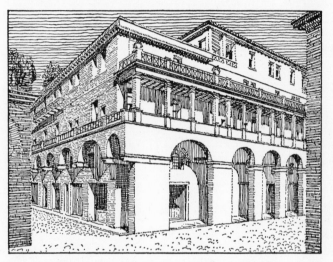

Flats and shops at Ostia near Rome (restored)

None of the ancient tenement-houses now exists in Rome itself; but at its former port of Ostia, 14 miles away, a tourist today can see many such, with balconies and staircases intact—all built of brick and concrete and quite surprisingly modern in appearance. Staircases at the side of the shops led up to residential "flats" above.

At Ostia there are few of the single-storey houses planned around an internal courtyard such as have been discovered at Pompeii (p. 17), though such houses still existed in Rome in numbers as late as A.D. 200, whereas most of the Ostian multi-storey houses are a century or so older. They are intermingled with commercial offices, warehouses and shops in the Roman way, there being no sharp distinction between the residential and commercial quarters, as in early Greek cities. Among the few large houses around internal courtyards may be mentioned the houses of Serapis and of the Charioteers.

The Porta Appia or San Sebastiano, Rome

From very early times Rome was a walled city; and even today a large part of its massive and lofty walls, with their towers and gateways, remains intact. In the remote days of the kings there was a small fortified nucleus, "Roma Quadrata," on the Palatine Hill, of which a few crumbling fragments have survived. Then the so-called "Servian Wall" was built, attributed to King Servius Tullius, 6th century B.C. It was some 8 miles in length and is believed to have enclosed a population of

about 80,000. For a portion of its length it followed the
bank of the Tiber. It was pierced by 17 gates. The few
portions still surviving (e.g. near the Central Railway
Station) are of no architectural interest.

The Porta Pinciana. In the old walls of Rome

The Aurelian Wall, erected during the third quarter of
the 3rd century A.D., was about 12 miles in length, and
was built at great speed by civilian labour directed by
military architects, under the threat of barbarian invasions. Its original height, 26 feet, was later doubled and
the walls were then provided with a gallery, a rampart
walk above and a crenellated parapet. Most of the 383
towers in its length were half round, but a few were
square on plan. Of its 18 gateways and 12 posterns about
half have now disappeared; but at least two gateways—
the Porta Appia or S. Sebastiano and the Porta Tibur-
tina—are still most imposing structures; and several of
the others (e.g. the Porta Pinciana), though smaller,
remain fairly intact. As will be noted in a later chapter
(p. 161), the clearance of this great girdle of walls from
the accretion of shacks and other unworthy buildings
which had grown up against them during the centuries

was one of the most welcome improvements in Rome effected between the two world wars.

Rome itself does not provide us with an example of successful town planning from classical times; for, as at Athens, the area around the monumental centre was occupied by inferior housing, and the famous roads converging, like the aqueducts, from all sides upon the city became lost in a jumble of mean streets within the walls; except only the Via Flaminia from the north, which was prolonged within the walls straight to the Capitol, on the line of the present Corso.

To find Italian towns consciously planned in Roman times one has to go north to Aosta or Turin, both founded by Augustus nearly 2,000 years ago. The nucleus of each town is a square, divided by straight narrow streets into small squares like a chessboard. Each square or "lot" (American) is called an *insula* (Lat. "island"). The town in each case is crossed at right angles by two wider main streets—the Decumanus, running east–west and bisecting the town, and the Cardo, running north–south. Scholars differ as to the origin of this somewhat unimaginative plan, some regarding it as a typical product of a military mind accustomed to planning a military camp. Whereas Aosta has remained a smallish town and has therefore felt no need to modify its original layout, Turin has grown into a large city (737,000 in 1951), but its original chessboard plan has been prolonged in all directions, so that almost all its extensive area is covered with rectangular *insulae* or "lots" today.

The Romans in their various buildings, as already noted, made constant use of the Orders of columns, adapted from Greek forms; and abreast of this trabeated construction of columns and beams (Lat. *trabs*, a beam) carried the development of arches and vaults to a high degree of efficiency, borrowing ideas from further east even if not from the Etruscans, as some scholars persist in believing. Their building materials have already been mentioned in Chapter 1, where the sources from which stone of various kinds, marble, timber and pozzolana were obtained have been indicated. The bricks which they used were much larger and thinner than those of today. (Examples may be seen in the Roman wall of the City of London, as well as at Verulamium and in the tower of St Albans Cathedral.)

The design of Roman buildings of any importance was carried out by professional architects, military or civil according to circumstances; and the helpful Vitruvius furnishes some information about their training and status. In the preface to his *De Architectura* he writes that: "Architects who have aimed at acquiring manual skill without scholarship have never been able to reach a position of authority to correspond with their pains, while those who relied only upon theories and scholarship were obviously hunting the shadow, not the substance. But those who have a thorough knowledge of both, like men armed at all points, have the sooner attained their object and carried authority with them." He outlines a desirable curriculum for a student of architecture: "Let him be educated, skilful with the pencil, know much history, have followed the philosophers with attention, understand music, have some knowledge of medicine, know the opinions of the jurists and be acquainted with astronomy and the theory of the heavens."

This somewhat staggering curriculum may be summarized as an education which gives due weight to the

D

humanities, the sciences and the fine arts, but seems to take a practical knowledge of construction for granted. At any rate, nobody has ever questioned the outstanding ability of Roman architects in that very important field; and it is from Roman structural skill that the whole of our Western Romanesque and Gothic architecture has sprung.

3

Early Christian Churches

DURING THE first three centuries of Christianity, from the date of Christ's crucifixion in *c.* A.D. 30 up to the time of the Emperor Constantine the Great, *c.* A.D. 287–337, who established toleration for Christians in 313 and was probably converted to Christianity in his last years, no churches are known to have been built in Italy or elsewhere. For much of this long period Christianity was proscribed, and its followers in Rome were persecuted with varying degrees of severity and cruelty, so that they were compelled to worship in secret, either in the catacombs or in private houses. Rome takes first place in this story, on account of its importance as the capital and the most populous city of the Empire, where, naturally, the first Christian churches came to be erected.

There is no need to minimize here the terrible conditions under which these early Christians suffered, or the surprising growth of their cult in such unfavourable circumstances. Modern novels such as *Ben Hur* may be highly coloured and over-dramatized; but no humane and intelligent visitor to the Colosseum can fail to imagine the horrible events that took place there before the emperor and the sadistically brutal concourse of Roman people, male and female. Among the long line of emperors, Tiberius (A.D. 14–37), Caligula (37–41) and Nero (54–68) at least fully justify their description as "monsters of iniquity"; and some of their ladies—Poppaea for one— were no better. Of the three men mentioned, Nero was perhaps the most evil and decadent and cruel. He dabbled in the arts, played his fiddle on one notable if legendary occasion, and built his famous "Golden House," the Domus Aurea, on the Palatine Hill. It was towards the end of his reign, in the year A.D. 67, that St Peter was crucified in Rome and St Paul was beheaded just outside its walls. The site of St Paul's execution is marked today by the Abbey of Tre Fontane ("Three Fountains" or "Springs"), where three fountains are said to have gushed out as the severed head hit the ground three times, and three churches now mark the places. As for the site of St Peter's execution in Nero's Circus on the Vatican Hill, that site is now occupied by the most famous Christian church in the world.

The catacombs have no architectural significance in the evolution of early church buildings. The Latin word *catacumbae* has a Greek origin (*kata*, down; *kumbē*, a hollow) and was applied to subterranean galleries hewn in the soft sandstone (near existing sand-pits or shallow quarries) for the burial of the dead. There are several groups of catacombs elsewhere than in Rome: at Naples, Syracuse and Palermo, in Tuscany and in Etruria—all in Italy; in Malta and at Alexandria, outside Italy; but those in Paris are more properly described as charnel-houses. Of the numerous Roman catacombs, all of which are outside the city walls, three groups are under the churches of S. Sebastiano nella Via Appia, S. Agnese *fuori* and S. Pancrazio. Of the other examples open to and usually visited by the public the chief are the catacombs of Callisto, Domitilla and Commodilla.

The earliest date from the 2nd century A.D., most of the others from the 3rd and 4th, after which inhumation in catacombs became rare and was replaced by burial in Christian churches. During the barbarian invasions of the "Dark Ages" almost all trace of the catacombs was lost until their accidental discovery by a studious monk in 1578. The various galleries, which total many miles in length, range in breadth from 3 to 4 feet and in height from 4 to 12 feet. The dead were buried in *loculi* (niches or recesses), arranged in tiers of five or more from floor to ceiling and closed by heavy stone slabs. The maze of galleries is varied by occasional large tombs (*cubicula*) where, in emergency, small gatherings for worship could have met; and the whole system is planned on different levels, with galleries crossing one another, and is provided with vertical shafts to admit light and air. A walk through these dark corridors is pathetic enough, with their innumerable inscriptions to the departed; but although some of the *cubicula* contain wall-paintings and could provide standing room for a few mourners, the catacombs were obviously the prototypes of the first Christian churches.

Of these latter Rome naturally contains the earliest and most famous examples, of which the following are the most notable:

1. *S. Agnese fuori le Mura* (St Agnes outside the Walls), founded by Constantine in 324, but largely rebuilt in 625–38 (see p. 51).

2. *S. Pietro in Vaticano* (St Peter's), founded by Constantine in 324 on the site of the Neronian Circus, and completely rebuilt in the 16th–17th centuries. "Old St Peter's" is described on pp. 46–7.

3. *S. Giovanni in Laterano* (St John Lateran), founded by Constantine in 330, but greatly altered in the 17th–18th centuries (pp. 47–8).

4. *S. Paolo fuori le Mura* (St Paul outside the Walls), founded in 380, destroyed by fire in 1823 and then rebuilt on the original lines (pp. 48–9).

5. *S. Sabina*, founded 425, and hardly altered since (p. 51).

6. *S. Maria Maggiore*, founded 432, but much altered in the 18th century, and with a campanile of 1377 (p. 49).

7. *S. Lorenzo fuori le Mura*, originally founded 330, rebuilt 432, and enlarged 579 (pp. 49–50).

To this list of early "basilican" churches must be added the circular church of S. Stefano Rotondo (470); the octagonal baptistery of Constantine (430–40); and the circular church of S. Costanza, the emperor's daughter (330), converted into a church in 1256 (p. 52). All these examples are in Rome; but there is another circular baptistery at Nocera, south of Naples (330).

A typical "basilican" church of the 4th–5th centuries usually had an aisled nave, separated from its flanking aisles by a range of columns. In the wall above them (later called the "clerestory") were round-headed windows to light the nave; at the east end was an apse; at the west end a narthex or vestibule; and sometimes there was a forecourt (*atrium* in Latin). The English term chancel is derived from Latin *cancelli* (barriers provided to protect the judge in the apse of a secular basilica from the public in the nave). In early Christian basilicas there was a range of seats round the apse for the bishop and officiating clergy, who thus had their backs to the east and faced the congregation. Normally there were no transepts, so the church was not cruciform in plan.

At first a small portable reading-desk or lectern

sufficed, but subsequently it was developed into an elaborate "three-decker" pulpit. This in turn was superseded by a pair of ambos or reading-desks (Latin plural of *ambo* is *ambones*): one on the south side for the gospel, the other on the north side for the epistle. There are several fine examples (in marble) in Rome and Ravenna. The first Christian altars were portable, thus resembling a "communion table" rather than a "stone of sacrifice." Another feature peculiar to these early churches was a *matroneum* (or women's gallery, from Latin *matrona*, a married woman). From the first days of worship in the catacombs the sexes were separated; and in "Old St Peter's" at Rome the left side of the nave was occupied by the men, the right by the women. Traces of wooden screens around the women's side have been found in some Italian churches. In S. Agnese fuori and in S. Lorenzo fuori, both at Rome, there are arched galleries for women overlooking the sanctuary and known as the *locus mulierum*. In the Roman churches of SS. Cosma e Damiano, S. Sebastiano fuori and S. Maria Maggiore, the *matroneum* consisted of a lower gallery surrounding and behind the apse, with windows looking into the sanctuary. There are also later examples in S. Ambrogio at Milan (p. 61) and St Mark's at Venice (pp. 66–8).

The "orientation" of buildings (Lat. *oriens, orientem*, the rising sun) means, in the case of a church, its siting with its main or longitudinal axis running east–west, and with its chancel (or presbytery) and its high altar at the east end; but this practice was by no means universal at all periods, and early Christian churches were "orientated" westwards, as the most renowned of them all—St Peter's at Rome—still is.

Beneath the high altar or the chancel a *confessio* was

often constructed, i.e. a crypt to contain the tomb of a saint or martyr. This feature exists at St Peter's, where there is also a fine *baldacchino* or isolated canopied structure over the high altar, but this is a work of the 17th century (p. 125). A less elaborate type of canopy, the ciborium, dating from the 9th century, may be seen in the church of S. Apollinare in Classe at Ravenna (p. 53). The picturesque brick *campanili* (plural of campanile) adjoining many churches in Rome, Ravenna and elsewhere are mostly of dates subsequent to the 6th century, the earliest use of a bell as a summons to Christian worship being recorded in 604. Thus none of the earliest basilican churches had either towers or domes.

Returning now to the famous churches listed on pp. 42-3, we may begin with "Old St Peter's," which was erected by Constantine approximately on the site of the present huge cathedral. He chose that site with a special purpose in his mind; for it was there that Nero's villa stood, with a circus in its grounds—the "Neronian Circus," where hundreds of Christians were tortured, crucified, burnt alive or thrown to the lions, as may be read on an inscription in the sacristy of the cathedral. Possibly St Peter, who was crucified in A.D. 67, was buried in the neighbouring cemetery. Recent excavation seems to confirm the idea that his tomb lay beneath the present crypt, and a tradition asserts that a small oratory was erected over the site by an early pope, long before Constantine's day.

At any rate there is no doubt at all about Constantine's great basilican church, "Old St Peter's," which was begun in A.D. 324, consecrated by Pope Sylvester I in 326, and completed in 349. It was planned parallel to the axial line of Nero's Circus, on which it abutted. Including its atrium, the whole length of the complex of buildings was about 800 feet, and the breadth over 200 feet. At the entrance on the east a great flight of steps led up to a portico and thence one entered a splendid colonnaded atrium. West of it lay the church itself, a noble five-aisled basilica of 380 feet by 212 feet, with an apse at its west end opening from a bema (transept) which was divided from the nave by an imposing arch. The high altar, beneath a ciborium or *baldacchino*, stood on the chord of the apse; and on a range of seats round the apse, behind the altar, sat the clergy, with the Pope himself in the centre, so that they looked down into the nave and faced east. The presbytery or chancel was enclosed by a low wall. The brick exterior walls of the Church were very plain, but internally the walls were decorated with mosaics and paintings. A crypt beneath the church contained the tombs of the early popes or "bishops of Rome," among them the first pope and bishop, St Peter, whose place of burial has been located with reasonable probability if not with absolute certainty by recent excavators and scholars. "Old St Peter's" with its mass of ancillary buildings was becoming ruinous in the 15th century, so Pope Nicholas V began the first part of the rebuilding (p. 90), which was continued until the early 17th century (pp. 101–3).

The Cathedral of St John Lateran ranks as "the cathedral of Rome and of the world" (Omnium urbis et orbis Ecclesiarum Mater et Caput) and here the popes were crowned up to 1870. Its name is derived from Plautius Lateranus, a rich patrician put to death by Nero. Founded in A.D. 330, it was burnt down and sacked by barbarians many times before it was rebuilt by Borromini *c.* 1650; and the dignified east end is a still later reconstruction of 1734–6, designed by Galilei (see pp. 130, 132). One way and another hardly anything remains of the original structure, but there is a beautiful 13th-century Romanesque cloister by the Cosmati, mentioned in my next chapter (pp. 78, 79).

S. Paolo fuori le Mura, or "St Paul outside the Walls," lies, as its name indicates, outside the Porta S. Paolo in the ancient city wall, on the south side of Rome. It is sometimes called the Basilica Ostiense because it adjoins the Via Ostiense, the road to Ostia; and it is, with the sole exception of St Peter's, the largest church in Rome. It is supposed to contain the tomb and body of St Paul, who was beheaded, as noted on p. 42, near the Abbey of Tre Fontane not far away in A.D. 67. Constantine erected a basilica here, which was enlarged in 386 by Theodosius, and after numerous vicissitudes was almost destroyed by fire in 1823. It was then completely rebuilt, and was consecrated by Pope Pius IX in 1854. Thus the building that we see today is modern and, moreover, work of a period now much out of fashion. Nevertheless it provides an excellent notion of what a typical basilican church of the grander sort must have looked like when it was brand-new, for the plan and arrangement of the original had been recorded and were carefully followed.

A visitor's first impression on approaching the church is usually unfavourable, for the *quadriporticus* or atrium by Giuseppe Sacconi (cf. p. 154), the mosaics of the façade, and the clumsy, inelegant 19th-century campanile all offend a sensitive eye. Once inside the building, however, the effect is very impressive, if somewhat garish; and the mosaics of the triumphal arch date from the 6th century, while those of the apse were executed by craftsmen *c.* 1220. The cloister, which luckily escaped damage in 1823, is a lovely work by the same master who was responsible for the cloister of St John Lateran in the early 13th century (cf. p. 78).

The great basilican church of S. Maria Maggiore is said by some critics to create a more accurate impression of its original form than any other of these early examples. Externally it is magnificent, but was entirely transformed into Late Renaissance form by Fuga, who designed the south-east façade in 1743, and by three other architects who designed the much more dignified apsidal end in the previous century. The fine medieval campanile, of arcaded brick, is the loftiest of its kind in Rome (cf. p. 62). The interior of the church is notable both for its great size, 280 feet long, and for its design. The massive marble and granite columns of the nave support an entablature adorned with mosaics, and above them are other mosaics of the 5th century. There are also medieval mosaics in the apse, a fine Cosmatesque marble pavement, and a handsome gilded ceiling of the 16th century.

Apart from these four great buildings there are several smaller basilican churches in the city which make a more intimate appeal to many visitors. S. Lorenzo fuori le Mura is indeed of considerable size, and of great interest. It was almost the only historical monument in Rome to suffer severe damage from bombing during the Second World War, when its proximity to the Central Railway Station may have provided the reason. The destruction was, however, limited in extent, and the church has since been restored with admirable skill and taste. One of the seven "pilgrimage churches" of Rome, it was founded by Constantine in A.D. 330, doubled in 432, rebuilt in 579, and much altered in 1216. The basilican interior has granite Ionic columns and fine mosaic decoration of the 12th century, earlier mosaics in the triumphal arch, a medieval bishop's throne, a Romanesque campanile, and a beautiful cloister of *c.* 1200. It has been mentioned already as containing a *matroneum* or women's gallery; and should be visited above all for the splendour and brilliance of its colouring, unsurpassed—since its post-war restoration—by any of the old basilicas in Rome. The adjoining Campo Verano was the place where many early Christian martyrs were buried, but is now a great modern cemetery full of bombastic memorials.

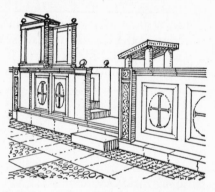

Ambo: The two ambones in the church
of S. Clemente, Rome (9th century)

San Clemente, near the Colosseum, was founded in A.D. 385, and has been described as "the most complete example in existence of the Christian basilica." This is true as far as its ritual arrangements are concerned; but only the "lower church" is of the date stated, the "upper church" being a work of 1108. Here we can see a Cosmatesque pavement, two ambones, a chancel screen with *transennae* (pierced ornamental openings), a chancel raised above a *confessio*, a high altar beneath a ciborium or

PLATE III

Rome: The Colosseum (*Photo: Richter*)

Rome: The Pantheon

PLATE IV

Rome: S. Sabina, interior

Rome: S. Constanza, interior (*Photo: Richter*)

baldacchino on marble columns, stalls for the clergy and a bishop's throne, as well as fine mosaics. Under the "lower church" is a pagan Mithraeum (temple of Mithras), and beneath that again—far below ground level—foundations of great antiquity.

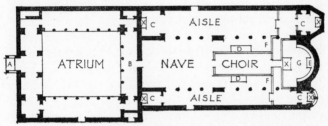

Plan of the Basilican Church of S. Clemente, Rome
A, Entrance; B, Narthex; C, Chapels; D, Ambos (pulpits);
E, Bishop's seat; F, Marble screens (Cancelli); G, Apse; X, Altars.

S. Sabina, near the Tiber, was built in A.D. 425, and is to my mind one of the most convincing of the basilican churches. It was well restored a few years ago. Its remarkable entrance door, of cypress wood, is carved with biblical scenes, and formed part of the original building. Though now lacking most of its former mosaic decorations, its austere interior is said to be the only remaining example in Rome of a basilica of the Ravenna type (cf. p. 53), with ranges of fine columns rifled from an older pagan temple.

S. Agnese fuori le Mura, on the north side of Rome, was originally built by Constantine in A.D. 324. St Agnes was a Christian maiden of Diocletian's time who was exposed naked in the Stadium, where according to tradition "her nakedness was covered by the miraculous growth of her hair." The fine Baroque church of S.

Agnese in the Piazza Navona (p. 129) marks the site of this miracle. She was then condemned to be burnt at the stake, but the flames refused to hurt her. Finally she was beheaded. The church of S. Agnese fuori, because it lies so far below street level, is approached down a flight of 45 marble steps, flanked by walls on which are sculptured the incidents of her martyrdom.

Close to this basilica is yet another of Constantine's buildings, the Mausoleum of S. Costanza, erected by him in 330 to the memory of his two daughters, Constantia (Costanza in Italian) and Helena (Elena in Italian). It is now a church, circular in plan, with a curiously shaped vestibule or porch. The domical roof is carried on two concentric rings of granite columns. The vault of the ambulatory between these columns and the circular outer walls is covered with very beautiful mosaics of the 4th century, representing supposedly biblical scenes such as the vintage.

Last among the Early Christian buildings of Rome must be mentioned the round church of S. Stefano Rotondo on the Coelian Hill, said to have been built in A.D. 468, but much altered since; indeed its present diameter is barely two-thirds of the original, the outer walls having been pulled down in 1450. Yet even as it stands it is one of the largest circular buildings in the world. There is some doubt as to its precise history, and modern visitors will probably be repelled by the hideously realistic scenes of martyrdom painted on its walls in the 17th century.

The importance of Rome as an administrative, religious and architectural centre was greatly diminished when Constantine transferred his capital in A.D. 328 from Rome to Byzantium (thereafter known as Constantinople), leaving Rome to become a secondary capital for the "Western Roman Empire"; but in A.D. 404 the Emperor Honorius made Ravenna his western capital instead of Rome. Thus the remaining Early Christian churches now to be described are all in or near Ravenna, on the north-west shore of the Adriatic. In 493 a Gothic invader named Theodoric proclaimed himself ruler of the new Visigothic "Kingdom of Italy," with Ravenna as his capital.

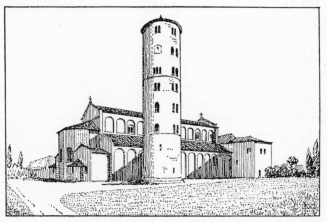

Ravenna: S. Apollinare in Classe: 534-49

In Ravenna itself these buildings comprise three churches and two tombs. Of the churches, S. Apollinare Nuovo (493-526) and S. Apollinare in Classe (534-49) are both of "basilican" type, with rows of antique marble columns supporting arcades of semicircular arches. Above these are a decorative frieze, a range of round-headed windows in a clerestory, and a timber roof which —in the case of S. Apollinare in Classe—is concealed by a panelled ceiling of 1611. Both contain magnificent contemporary mosaics. These two churches exhibit certain special features of interest, some of which are of oriental origin, so that the buildings are generally described as "Byzantine" rather than "Early Christian." The name Classe is the Italian equivalent of the Latin *classis*, a fleet, and S. Apollinare in Classe, now standing solitary and forlorn in a marsh near the sea and adjoining a lovely *pineta* (cf. p. 7), marks the site of a famous Adriatic port founded by Augustus. Thus Eastern influence from Syria and Byzantium found ready access here.

Specifically Byzantine architectural features are the beautiful "wind-blown" acanthus leaves of the capitals over the columns; the pulvins or dosserets (cushion-shaped blocks) above the capitals, from which the arches spring; the polygonal exterior of the apse; and the design of the mosaics. Each church has a curious cylindrical campanile of later date, perhaps first intended as a watch-tower; but it is generally considered that the use of bells as a summons to Christian worship was first introduced at Ravenna in 604.

Of a very different type is the celebrated church of S. Vitale at Ravenna (526–47). It is octagonal in general plan, with a domed central space surrounded by a galleried ambulatory. Nothing quite like it had ever been seen in Italy before. From the octagon project an apse and a narthex or porch. The dome rises from an elaborate arrangement of eight arches. Though some later sculptural additions have marred the harmony of the interior, it remains one of the most interesting and important churches in all Italy, and is justly famous for the splendour of its mosaic decorations.

The other buildings of this period in Ravenna are the tombs of Galla Placidia (450) and of King Theodoric or

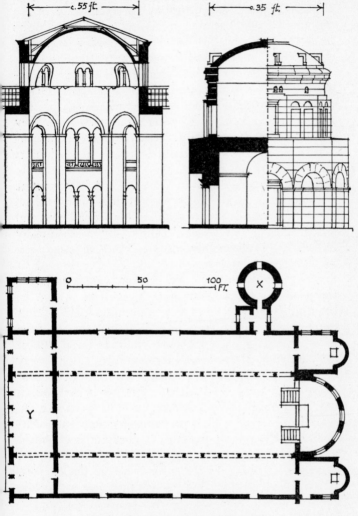

Early Christian buildings in Ravenna
Top left: Central dome of S. Vitale. Top right: Tomb of Theodoric.
Below: Plan of S. Apollinare in Classe. X, Campanile. Y, Narthex.

E

Theoderic (526), which are of no significance in the history of Early Christian architecture; but Theodoric's tomb is an amazing feat of construction, for its slightly convex "lid" or flat dome or roof consists of a single block of limestone over 35 feet in diameter, hollowed out beneath like an inverted saucer, but nevertheless estimated to weigh 200 tons. These architects of the 6th century in Ravenna must have been ingenious people, for they constructed the dome of S. Vitale entirely of earthenware pots, interlocking like modern socketed drainpipes for the sake of lightness.

Also within the radius of Ravenna and its Byzantine influences was the neighbouring province of Istria, which has in turn formed part of Austria, Italy, Yugoslavia and Trieste during the present century, but is historically Italian. The basilican church at Grado, on an island west of Trieste, was built in 571–86; and the fine example at Parenzo, south-west of Trieste and easily accessible therefrom by frequent steamers, dates from 535–43. Its beautiful situation close to the sea, and the admirable condition in which it has been maintained, make it one of the most interesting Early Christian churches for a visit, as it retains all its original ritual arrangements, a fine display of mosaics, a baptistery, a narthex and an atrium. Not many miles away, at Aquileia, is another large basilican church of still more ancient date; but it has been so often altered and repaired after numerous invasions and earthquakes in the remote past that it does not compare in interest with the Early Christian churches of Rome, Ravenna, Grado and Parenzo described in this chapter. Neither Aquileia nor Grado suffered damage during the Second World War, but the two basilican churches in Ravenna sustained minor casualties.

4

Romanesque Architecture

c. 568 – c. 1200

THE TERM Romanesque is now generally used to describe all those architectural features, particularly structural forms, in Western, Central and Northern Europe
which were derived from Roman as opposed to "Byzantine" architecture, originating at Byzantium or Constantinople. Thus "Romanesque" covers "Saxon" and
"Norman" architecture in England, "Rhenish" architecture in Germany and "Lombard" architecture in
Italy; but in north-eastern Italy, especially in Venetia, a
hybrid style arose which has sometimes been called
"Byzantine-Romanesque," e.g. at St Mark's, Venice
(p. 66–8).

The date chosen here for its beginning, A.D. 568,
marked the establishment of the Lombard kingdom of
Italy, which lasted till 774, when the Lombard king
Desiderius was deposed by his son-in-law, Charlemagne,
king of the Franks, who was crowned as the "Holy
Roman Emperor" by Pope Leo III in 774. A few years
earlier, in 756, Charlemagne's father, Pepin, had defeated
the Lombards, who had then been forced to yield

Ravenna, the Duchy of Spoleto and parts of the Romagna to the Pope, thus founding the temporal sovereignty of the Papacy in the territory thereafter known as the "Papal States" or the "States of the Church" or the "Patrimony of St Peter."

From that date much of northern and central Italy, from the Alps in the north to a line across the peninsula marked by the River Liris or Garigliano, about 50 miles south-west of Rome (approximately the boundary of the present province of Lazio, Latium in Latin), formed part of the Empire, under the name of the "Kingdom of Italy," which lasted—under that title—till 961. South of this line lay the former Lombard duchy of Benevento and the possessions of the Byzantine emperor, which also included Venice, Istria, Sicily and Sardinia. These two islands then came under the rule of the Muslims or "Saracens" for a time, with a marked effect on their subsequent architecture, as will shortly be explained; and then southern Italy and Sicily were acquired by Norman adventurers who first made themselves "counts of Apulia" (the "heel" of Italy) and next, in 1061–90, conquered the whole of Sicily. They in their turn introduced their native "Norman" or "Romanesque" architecture. In 1194 these Norman rulers were defeated and deposed by the Holy Roman Emperor. It was about this time, c. 1200, that Romanesque architecture slowly and reluctantly gave place to Gothic, but the change was so gradual, and varied so much in different parts of Italy, that no definite date can be assigned for it.

The so-called "Lombard" architecture that prevailed in northern and central Italy for some two or three centuries derives its name from the Longobards or Langobardi (= long-beards) or Lombards, a Suevic tribe from

East Germany, who had progressively moved from Eastern Europe to the lower Elbe in North Germany during the 1st century, to the Danube in the 4th–5th centuries, to Pannonia (Hungary) in the 6th, and thence entered Italy via the Julian Alps in 568, giving their name to "Lombardy." They were converted to Christianity and established their capital at Pavia, on the River Po near Milan, in 572.

It has been said that during the period of their rule, from 568 to 774, Italian art sank to the lowest level that it ever reached. Certainly the Lombards, at the time of their arrival in Italy, were a very savage race, but soon after that date they had evidently begun to take notice of the fine buildings already existing there, and as early as the last years of the 6th century their queen Theodelinda was erecting churches at Pavia, Cremona and Bergamo; also a fine basilica at Monza (595, since destroyed), where she rebuilt Theodoric's summer palace.

The only surviving buildings in Italy of the Lombard period, i.e. before 774, are the nave and eastern part of S. Pietro at Toscanella, some 50 miles north-west of Rome (739, the west end being later); S. Salvatore at Brescia in Lombardy (753); and S. Maria in Cosmedin at Rome (772–95), but this last was only an enlargement of a much earlier church, and was again extensively altered in the 9th and 10th centuries. As it stands, it is an excellent specimen of a medieval Roman church, and has a fine brick campanile of seven stages or storeys, but of 12th- or 13th-century date (see p. 63). From the 9th century may be dated the churches of S. Maria in Domnica, Rome (817); S. Prassede, Rome (822, on the site of an older church); and S. Giorgio in Velabro, Rome (possibly 827–49, but this seems doubtful); also S. Pietro at Agliate near Monza in Lombardy (*c.* 875); and perhaps the campanile of S. Satiro, Milan (*c.* 876).

It does not seem likely that the Lombards themselves can have brought with them from Germany any useful ideas on architectural design; indeed Charlemagne, although a patron of the arts, had produced very little in his German dominions except the Dom at Aachen (796–804), which is generally regarded today as an imitation of S. Vitale at Ravenna (cf. pp. 54–5). It has been suggested that the Lombards availed themselves of the talents of the so-called "Comacine masters" for the design and decoration of their churches. Very little is known of the Magistri Commacini or Comacini, except that they were granted the privileges of freemen in the Lombard kingdom. While some authorities derive their name from an island (Isola Comacina) in Lake Como, others rashly trace it to *co-maciones*, i.e. members of a guild of masons, from Lower Latin *macio*. All this is very conjectural, and we can only assume safely that the Lombards did utilize the services of skilled craftsmen whom they found working in Italy.

The two major buildings of the Lombard Romanesque period in Italy are the churches of S. Michele at Pavia, the first Lombard capital, and S. Ambrogio at Milan, which later became the capital of Italy.

Pavia is not much visited today by tourists, but still preserves a few of the hundred stark and lofty watch-towers which earned its ancient nicknames of *civitas centum turrium* and *civitas turrigera*; and a very picturesque covered bridge across the River Ticino—badly damaged during an air-raid in 1944. The Duomo or Cathedral of S. Michele is a massive, vaulted, cruciform building with an eastern apse, and was erected in 1117–32. S. Zeno at

Verona has a somewhat similar arrangement, and is of uncertain date (11th–12th centuries), but its fine Romanesque portal was added in 1139.

S. Ambrogio at Milan is one of the famous churches of Italy. The original building, erected in the 9th century, was of the normal basilican type with aisles and an open timber roof. Of that building the triple apse, the crypt and the south campanile were preserved when the church was remodelled in the late 11th century to allow of a vaulted roof being substituted. The eight bays of the nave were then reduced to four square bays, divided by massive piers to carry the arched ribs of the main vault, which had the considerable span of 38 feet. The aisles, which were also vaulted, were raised to form buttresses to resist the outward thrust of the heavy nave vault. In front of the church itself is a vaulted atrium; and a north campanile was added to balance that on the south. The importance of these two churches is that they were vaulted at so early a date (cf. the earliest notable example in England—Durham Cathedral nave, 1128–33). Unfortunately S. Ambrogio suffered severely in the Second World War, especially the vaulting and the mosaics. The urge to provide fireproof roofs to churches was originally caused by the raids and burnings of the Saracens and the Normans, but vaulting was of little avail against aerial bombs in 1944.

Another church in Lombardy, the cathedral at Novara, built in the 10th century as a basilica of the normal type with low-pitched timber roofs, was reroofed in the 11th century with ribbed vaulting carried on compound piers, as at S. Ambrogio just described.

Of the early Romanesque churches of Lombardy it may be said in general that they were the first buildings in which vaulting had been used since ancient Roman days, but the same statement applies to certain buildings in northern France where Roman remains existed to serve as models. In Lombardy most of the surviving Romanesque examples are of basilican type, with apses at the east end of the nave and both aisles, rubble stone walls, a timber roof, and round-headed windows set centrally in the thickness of the walls. Externally walls were divided into bays by narrow strips or pilasters, terminating just below the projecting eaves or parapet in a row of small arches, used decoratively to form a cornice. Gables, low in pitch, were treated in the same way.

Campanili, usually square on plan, are divided into stages or storeys by horizontal bands and rows of small arches; and windows are provided in some of the storeys, grouped as two-, three- or four-light windows in a carefully graded scheme of fenestration. There are many such *campanili* attached to or adjoining Romanesque churches in Rome, e.g. SS. Giovanni e Paolo, S. Francesca Romana, S.M. in Cosmedin, S. Giorgio in Velabro, S.M. in Trastèvere—all of the 12th century or thereabouts, and built of brick with horizontal bands of marble moulding.

In Emilia, the Italian province adjoining Lombardy, there are great Romanesque cathedrals at Modena, 1099–1184; Parma, 1106, rebuilt after an earthquake in 1117; Piacenza, 1122–58 and later; and Borgo San Donnino, probably 12th century. It has been suggested that some inspiration for these remarkable buildings was derived from the basilican church of S. Miniato at Florence, rebuilt in 1013. This has an open timber roof and a curiously classical façade. A notable feature is the great height of the chancel floor, which is raised 11 feet above the floor of the nave, over a vaulted crypt.

Rome: S. Maria in Cosmedin

At Pisa, which is not far from the great quarries of white marble at Carrara, the chief medieval buildings are faced internally and externally with white and grey marble in alternate stripes. The cathedral, begun in 1063 after Pisa had captured Palermo in Sicily and was very prosperous, is a large cruciform church with double aisles on either side of the nave, apsidal transepts, an eastern apse, and a curious elliptical dome over the crossing. Its architect's name was Buschetto. The internal mosaics are of much later date. The adjoining baptistery, begun ninety years later, was so long in building that its upper part was enriched with crocketed gables and a gallery in the new Gothic fashion of the 13th century.

The famous campanile, commonly called the "Leaning Tower of Pisa," was begun c. 1174, on pile foundations in view of its marshy site, but had started to lean when it had risen only 35 feet above the ground. The work was then suspended for a while, but was resumed in the Gothic period, when three more stages were daringly added. Nevertheless it still stands—a source of anxiety to its guardians; and its top, 178 feet high, overhangs its base by 14 feet. One distinguished architectural historian, Sir Thomas Jackson, writing in 1920, made this extraordinary comment: "Here the Pisans have indulged to the full their passion for arcading, with a magnificent result. At the same time, strange as it may seem, I think the effect owes something to the accident of the tower leaning out of the perpendicular. Had it been upright, I am not sure that all those arcades in contiguity to the multitudinous arcading of the Duomo would have pleased so well; there would have been too much of them; whereas the inclination gives them a fresh aspect." My only comment on this pronouncement is that there is no accounting for tastes!

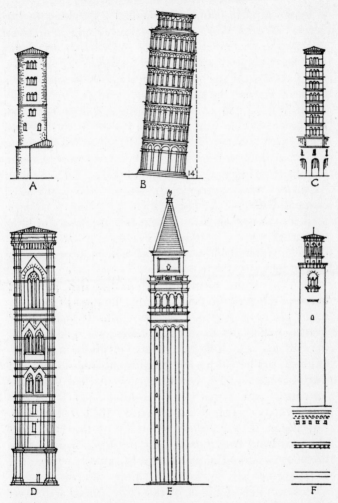

Campanili: A, S. Apollinare in Classe, Ravenna (6th century); B, "the Leaning Tower," Pisa (1174); C, S. Maria in Cosmedin, Rome (12th century); D, "Giotto's Tower," Florence (1334); E, S. Marco, Venice (902, rebuilt after 1902); F, Palazzo del Signore, Verona (1172 onwards).

In the terrible damage wrought by bombing in the Second World War, although most of the numerous churches in Pisa suffered severely and a large part of the city was utterly devastated, the cathedral escaped with two shell-holes in the roof, the baptistery with one broken column, and the "Leaning Tower"—amazing to relate—stood firm, in spite of one direct hit. On the other hand the lovely Gothic Campo Santo (= cemetery) adjoining the cathedral was so seriously damaged that the sober report of the British Committee on "The Preservation of Works of Art in Italy," published in 1945, describes it as "a major artistic disaster of the war"; for its walls were covered with fine frescoes which were ruined when a shell set the roof on fire. Fortunately the beautiful little Gothic church of S. Maria della Spina (p. 80) escaped damage. Another Romanesque church of importance in central Italy is S. Frediano at Lucca, 1112–47.

In Venetia the form of architecture that prevailed between the 7th century and the beginnings of Gothic (*c.* 1200) has been described as "Byzantine Romanesque." Venice itself began to rise on piles from a mud-bank in the Adriatic as a result of barbarian invasions in the 5th–6th centuries by Goths, Huns and Lombards in turn; and there—as Cassiodorus wittily wrote—the first Venetians "squatted and rested like sea-fowl." Their earliest churches have perished, but the great cathedral of St Mark was begun in 929 to receive relics of the Evangelist obtained from Alexandria in Egypt. It was damaged by fire in 976, restored, and then, *c.* 1063, entirely remodelled as a five-domed Byzantine building, almost certainly copied from the Church of the Holy Apostles at Constantinople (destroyed in 1463). As we see St Mark's today, with its florid and gorgeously decorated front

PLATE V

Lecce: SS. Nicolo e Cataldo, Norman doorway (*Photo: Alinari*)

PLATE VI

Siena: Cathedral, exterior (*Photo by courtesy of the Italian State Tourist Office*)

towards the Piazza, it is difficult to realize how simple and
dignified is the structure behind the façade, but internally,
in spite of the blaze of mosaics, the design is more

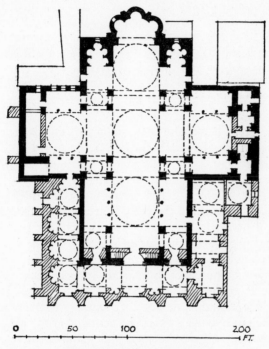

0   50   100   200 FT.

St Mark's Venice: Ground Plan

Walls of original building are shown above in solid
black; additions are hatched.

apparent. Originally its plain brick walls and depressed
hemispherical domes were all visible, externally and internally; but as soon as the main structure was completed
its decoration with marble and mosaic—inside and outside

—was hurried forward, Greek artists being hired from Constantinople. A large proportion of the marble details were obtained, however, from the ruins of neighbouring towns destroyed by Attila the Hun and other pagan invaders—notably from Aquileia (which is said to have boasted 600,000 inhabitants at one time, and has now almost vanished). It took 200 years to decorate St Mark's; and the gaudy and riotous crocketing over the main portals in the Piazza is late Gothic work of the 14th century. St Mark's, except for this last aberration, is a purely Byzantine church.

The great brick campanile adjoining the cathedral is 322 feet high. It was built in 888, collapsed and was rebuilt in 1329; collapsed again in 1902 and was rebuilt for the second time between 1902 and 1912.

Outside Venice itself the cathedral of Torcello was originally founded in the 7th century; was altered in 864 when the tribune, crypt and eastern apses were built; and was again partly reconstructed in 1001–8. Near it is the small church of S. Fosca, remodelled c. 1008; and not far away is the church of Burano. In spite of such characteristic Romanesque features as rows of external arcading, these churches all possess Byzantine characteristics; and the same tendency may be observed at the abbey of Pomposa, at distant Ancona, and perhaps even so far down the Adriatic coast as Brindisi. Examples of "Byzantine Romanesque" in the secular architecture of Venice are the Fondaco dei Turchi (probably 11th century) and the Palazzo Loredan—both on the Grand Canal. None of the Venetian buildings mentioned above suffered damage in the Second World War.

In southern Italy and Sicily external influences upon the development of Romanesque architecture were contributed by Muslim (or "Moorish" or "Saracen") invaders from North Africa and Spain (cf. p. 8) and by Norman invaders from the north. The forays of these two groups of alien conquerors covered almost exactly the period of Romanesque architecture; for, at the time when the Gothic phase began (c. 1200) in Italy, all that country, including the Pope's temporal dominions, had become part of the "Holy Roman Empire," and all the invaders had been banished.

In the beginning, c. 750, the "Saracen" dominions comprised the whole of North Africa and Western Asia, from the Atlantic to the Indus (except Asia Minor, which was held by the Byzantine emperor), and also the whole of Spain and Portugal. All this vast territory of the Muslim Caliphate had been conquered by the Arabs since Muhammad's death in 632. Saracen raids on Sicily and the coasts of southern Italy began with the landing of a large Muslim army in 827. They captured successively Girgenti, Palermo in 832, the great city of Syracuse in 878, and soon afterwards became masters of the whole of Sicily except the north-east tip near Mount Etna. Sicily became a Muslim emirate under the Fatimite rulers of Egypt.

The Norman adventurers Robert and Roger de Hauteville, sons of Tancred of Hauteville in Normandy, had been preceded by elder brothers who had already established themselves in southern Italy as counts of Apulia, dukes of Benevento and feudatories of the Holy Roman Empire. One of these elder brothers, Geoffrey or Godfrey, became the first Count of Lecce (cf. pp. 145-7). Robert and Roger embarked upon the conquest of Sicily in 1061, and completely achieved it in 1090. Finally one of Roger's sons, "Count Roger II," was crowned as the first King of Sicily in 1130, and his family held the island until 1194.

Romanesque buildings in southern Italy (excluding Sicily) include the cathedrals of S. Maria Maggiore at Siponto near Manfredonia (early 12th century), and of Trani, Bitonto, Bari, Otranto and Troia (12th–13th centuries). The cathedral of Salerno (1070) is noted for its pulpit and other inlaid work of *c.* 1175, and was slightly damaged in the Second World War; but the cathedral at Aversa near Naples, with its fine apses and chevet, fortunately escaped. The town of Aversa, founded in 1029, was the first Norman settlement in southern Italy.

Other "Norman" Romanesque churches include S. Nicola at Bari and SS. Niccolo e Cataldo at Lecce (1180), with a richly ornamented western doorway. Most of the inlaid or Cosmatesque mosaic work found in southern Italy (e.g. at Caserta Vecchia, Ravello, Sessa Aurunca) is of somewhat later date and is referred to in my next chapter. The Cosmati, as explained therein, and the less-known Vassalletti were groups of craftsmen who worked in Italy during the 13th century (p. 78). Some scholars object to the attribution of credit for designing the Romanesque churches to the Norman invaders, arguing that these buildings were part of the general native evolution of Italian Romanesque art.

In Sicily, on the other hand, the credit must be shared between the Norman conquerors and their "Saracen" predecessors who had occupied the island for 200 years previously; and indeed the character of Sicilian Romanesque buildings, as well as historical records, proves that "Saracen" architects had much to do with their design and decoration. In particular the pointed arch—which in Northern Europe first appears in the late 12th century and heralds the beginnings of the Gothic style—is found at a much earlier date in Sicily. The explanation is that in

England and France its ancestry goes back to the Crusaders, who found pointed arches as old as the 9th century in Egypt (e.g. in the mosque of Ibn Tulun at Cairo), and brought home this novel idea; whereas the Sicilian architects—probably Arab by birth—were already familiar with this structural form in North Africa and other Muslim lands, and carried it across the narrow Sicilian Channel.

Conditions in Sicily during the years of the Norman conquest (1061–90) and for some time afterwards were naturally most unfavourable for architectural progress; and all the innumerable mosques alleged to have been erected by the "Saracens"—three hundred in Palermo according to one imaginative Arab chronicler in 962—have disappeared long ago. Yet many of the distinctive features of Muslim art appear in the churches and other buildings erected after the conquest, e.g. stilted and pointed arches, crenellated parapets, pierced window-slabs (*transennae*), domes on pendentives, interlacing patterns of great intricacy, even the curious Muslim "stalactite ornament."

The principal Sicilian Romanesque churches surviving today are either "domical" or "basilican," but the latter type sometimes has a dome over the crossing and always a hemispherical dome over the eastern apse. The former group includes a very small and early building, S. Giovanni dei Leprosi, Palermo, of orthodox Christian type, built by Robert Guiscard in 1071 and domed; the Cappella Palatina, Palermo (1132); S. Giovanni degli Eremiti, Palermo (1132–48, with five domes); La Martorana, Palermo (1143, domed); Cefalù Cathedral (1129–1148); S. Cataldo, Palermo (1161, three domes); Monreale Cathedral (1172); Palermo Cathedral (1185, greatly

F

altered in later years); and the Palace of La Cuba, Palermo (1185). All these buildings, early as many of them are, have pointed arches; and the combination of Eastern domes and stilted arches with Romanesque features gives most of them a somewhat oriental aspect. All those mentioned above escaped damage in the Second World War, though many other churches in Palermo suffered severely.

There are many examples of fine mosaic decorations of the 12th century in Sicily, especially on the walls of the Cappella Palatina (1132 onwards) and the vault of La Martorana, both in Palermo; the walls of Monreale Cathedral (1172–90); and the apse of Cefalù Cathedral.

5

Gothic Architecture

c. 1200 – *c.* 1430

TASTE IN ARCHITECTURE has always been liable to changes of fashion, and, as readers will be aware, the "Gothic Revival" of the 19th century, in all European countries as in their colonies and in the United States, held the field during the first fifty years or so of Victoria's glorious reign. It was aided and popularized by the mellifluous and sonorous prose of Ruskin, who published *The Poetry of Architecture* in 1839 when he was only 19, *The Seven Lamps of Architecture* in 1849 and *The Stones of Venice* in 1851–3. Nobody has ever questioned his brilliance as a writer; but as a critic of architecture his views have lost much of their original force, and some of them are now generally considered to have been—in the words of recent scholars—"dull," "prejudiced," "arrogant," "peevish" and "ineffectual." Without presuming to offer an opinion on this matter, it may fairly be said that, while he did acquaint his large public with some knowledge and understanding of Gothic architecture in Italy and elsewhere, his didactic and contemptuous treatment of the classical and Renaissance period detracted

73

greatly from the value of his confident assertions. To him
the Renaissance was "a foul torrent"—just that! (Admittedly it is an acquired taste.)

Attempting to look more dispassionately today at
Italian Gothic architecture, one finds that most reputable
scholars during the last fifty years or more are unanimous
in their view that it is inferior in character and quality to
the Gothic of France and England. As for German Gothic,
that was a derivative of French, and Spanish Gothic was
inspired by German and French. Italian Gothic had many
distinctive features not found in any of the countries
mentioned; and this chapter must begin with some
account of those features in comparison with the coeval
work of England and France.

At the outset the origin of the familiar English word
Gothic must be explained. It was first used in the 17th
century, and was as much a term of abuse as "Vandal,"
which had a common origin. It was erroneously supposed
that the Goths and Vandals between them had destroyed
the classical monuments of Imperial Rome, which was
perhaps an excusable assumption, although in fact the
Goths and Vandals did not destroy any great buildings
during their invasions of Italy: the collapse of those
buildings was due to subsequent neglect and decay during
the "Dark" and Middle Ages. It was, however, quite
unjustifiable to describe the architecture of the Middle
Ages as "Gothic" (a nickname or term of opprobrium)
simply because Wren and his contemporaries regarded it
as "barbarous," seeing that neither Goths nor Vandals
had ever created any architecture worthy of mention![1]

Today "Gothic" has become a precise and recognized
term in architecture, and most certainly not a term of

[1] On all this see my book *Goths and Vandals* (1952).

abuse. The historical limits of the style in Italy may be very approximately dated as 1200–1430; but some Romanesque features may be found after 1200, and the architectural Renaissance began in Florence before 1420, while Milan Cathedral (Gothic) was not finished till 1485.

In North European countries the pointed arch is considered to be the hallmark of Gothic, and on the Italian mainland is a fairly safe guide; but in Sicily, as noted in my previous chapter, it was introduced at a much earlier date by architects from North Africa, where it had long been in use before the Crusaders brought it to Northern Europe in the 12th century or thereabouts. Hence we find it at Cefalù and in several churches at Palermo (p. 71). Moreover, the use of round arches continued in Italy abreast of the new pointed type, for the classical tradition remained very strong almost up to the beginning of the Renaissance, which naturally germinated in very receptive soil.

When Italian Gothic did evolve, its growth and development were slow and half-hearted, again owing to the persistence of Roman and Romanesque tradition; and in Sicily the "Saracenic" influence was potent. Whereas the whole effect of Northern Gothic churches was vertical, in Italy the use of horizontal mouldings and low-pitched roofs continued. The outstanding feature of Northern Gothic is its system of skeleton-construction, in which the weight of the (usually) vaulted roofs is transmitted by stone ribs on to regularly spaced piers and buttresses instead of on to thick walls, so that the thin walls between the buttresses can be pierced for large windows —traceried in late work; with the result that in very late Northern Gothic buildings (e.g. King's College Chapel, Cambridge) the whole structure consists of very slender stone piers, elaborate buttresses, and vaulting ribs, with an enormous area of stained glass.

This form of construction—Gothic carried to its logical sequel—is seldom found in Italy. The piers in the arcades of the larger churches (e.g. the Duomo at Florence) are more massive and more widely spaced; external walls are thicker; buttresses play little part in the scheme; stained glass is infrequent and unimportant. The triforium and clerestory, such prominent features in the interior of French and English cathedrals, have little significance in Italian examples.

Most of the famous Gothic cathedrals of Northern Europe are of grey stone, though Chester, Carlisle and a few others are of red sandstone. In Italy many of the largest and most important (e.g. Milan, Siena, Orvieto) are faced with white and coloured marbles, although the actual walls may be of brick; and in some cases this rough brickwork is still visible, the marble facing never having been added. There are also many large brick-Gothic churches in Italy, especially in the plains of Lombardy where good building stone is scarce; but one must remember that there are several magnificent brick-Gothic cathedrals in North Germany, and a few brick-Gothic churches in Essex (England), to say nothing of a single belated brick-Gothic example in America—St Luke's Church, Virginia (1632), erected soon after the first British settlement there.

The startling—and to some eyes blatant and strident—horizontal stripes of alternate white and dark marble on the walls of some Gothic churches in central Italy are sometimes attributed to "Saracenic" influence; but the "Saracens" themselves—wild untutored nomads originally—almost certainly borrowed the idea from the Byzantine habit of building walls in alternating layers of brick and stone. Something similar, and still older, may be seen in the Roman wall of the City of London, where horizontal bands or "lacing courses" of brickwork are used at intervals in a wall of rubble stone.

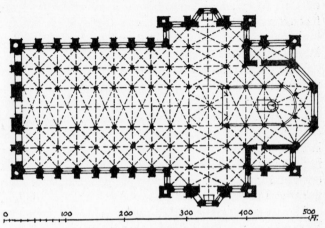

Milan Cathedral: Ground Plan

Some of these Italian churches (e.g. Orvieto Cathedral) have a façade bearing little relation to the actual structure of the building; others, in white marble, are reminiscent of iced wedding-cakes. The early Gothic church of S. Francesco at Assisi (begun in 1228) is much more akin, in sober colouring as in design, to Northern Gothic. The explanation usually offered is that its architect was a German (as was the alleged designer of Milan Cathedral); but M. Corroyer, as a patriotic Frenchman, will have none of this.[1]

As for Milan Cathedral, it is of course one of the most

[1] E. Corroyer, *L'Architecture gothique* (1891).

famous in Europe, and in point of mere size it is surpassed among medieval churches only by that of Seville.
Externally it displays a riot of white marble pinnacles;
internally it is more sombre and impressive, with gigantic piers 60 feet high supporting a vault which rises 145
feet above the floor. Yet it lacks the dignity and the
logical design of the more austere Gothic cathedrals of
France and England.

Window tracery never developed far in Italy, and shafts
with small arches above them separated the "lights" as in
Romanesque windows; whereas in England and France
slender moulded mullions took their place. Circular windows ("rose windows" or "wheel windows") continued
in fashion through the Gothic period. The fanciful tracery
in the arches of the Doge's Palace at Venice may well have
derived some of its exuberance from "Saracenic" influence, as also the crested parapets on the same building.

The groups of craftsmen known as the Cosmati and the
Vassalletti worked in central Italy through the 13th century on marble and glass mosaic. Their delicate designs
are to be seen in the cloisters of S. Giovanni in Laterano
and of S. Paolo fuori (both 1219–21), in the pulpits and
ambones of S.M. Ara Coeli, S. Clemente and S. Lorenzo
fuori—all these in Rome; in the porch of the cathedral of
Città Castellana (1210) near Rome; and even on two
tombs in Westminster Abbey. Another famous work of
craftsmanship is Giovanni Pisano's carved pulpit (1302) in
the cathedral of Pisa.

Domestic architecture in the Italian Gothic style is seen
at its best in many palaces still standing in Venice and
Siena. The numerous examples in the beautiful little town
of Viterbo, north of Rome, suffered terribly in the Second
World War. The following chronological list of the

principal Gothic buildings in Italy provides an introduction to the standard topographical guide-books. It will be noted that Rome itself furnishes only one example, the church of S.M. sopra Minerva, which was heavily restored in 1847 (when all the Baroque decorations were removed, with the pious intention of re-creating its original effect—possibly a trifle too colourful for Northern eyes). Buildings in this list which were severely damaged in the Second World War include S. Francesco and S.M. della Verità at Viterbo; S. Trinità and S. Croce at Florence; and the Ponte Scaligero at Verona.

Thirteenth Century

1208	Fossanova (60 m. S. of Rome). Cistercian abbey (pointed arches)
1210	Città Castellana. Porch of the cathedral, by the Cosmati
1215	Como. The Broletto (round and pointed arches)
1217	Casamari. S. of Rome. Cistercian abbey (pointed arches)
1218 on	S. Galgano, near Siena. Cistercian abbey (pointed arches)
1219	Vercelli (Piedmont). S. Andrea (round and pointed arches)
1219–21	Rome. S. Giovanni in Laterano, cloister; by the Cosmati
,,	Rome. S. Paolo fuori, cloister; by the Cosmati
1228–32	Assisi. S. Francesco (see also 1253)
1236	Viterbo. S. Francesco; altered 1373
1245–1380	Siena. Cathedral (consecrated 1267; W. front 1284)
1247	Viterbo. Palazzo Comunale; enlarged 1448
13th c.	,, Palazzo Papale and Loggia Papale
,,	,, S. Maria del Paradiso, cloister
13th–14th c.	,, S.M. della Verità, now Museo Civico

1250–1338	Venice. Church of the Frari
c. 1250–1335	,, SS. Giovanni e Paolo
1250 on	Florence. S. Trinità rebuilt
c. 1250	,, The Bargello
1253	Assisi. Upper church of S. Francesco (see also 1228)
1260	Pisa. Upper part of baptistery
1278	,, Campo Santo
1278–1348	Florence. S.M. Novella
c. 1280	Rome. S. Maria sopra Minerva
1288–1309	Siena. Palazzo della Signoria (Palazzo Pubblico)
1290–1309	Orvieto Cathedral
1294	Florence. S. Croce; by Arnolfo
,,	,, Cathedral of S.M. del Fiore; by Arnolfo
1298	,, Palazzo Vecchio; by Arnolfo

Fourteenth Century

1307	Genoa. S. Lorenzo remodelled
1323	Pisa. Cappella della Spina remodelled
1334	Florence. "Giotto's Campanile"
1337–1404	,, S.M. di Or S. Michele (S. Michele in Orto)
1340–1404	Venice. Ducal Palace; sea front
1348	Asti. Cathedral
1354	Verona. Ponte Scaligero
1370	Chiaravalle. Central cupola and tower
1387–1485	Milan Cathedral

Fifteenth Century

Early 15th c.	Viterbo. Palazzo Farnese
,,	Venice. Palazzo Pisani
1424	,, Ducal Palace; front to the Piazzetta, by G. and B. Bon
1430	,, Ca d'Oro ("Golden House")
1448–56	Udine. Palazzo del Comune

Mixed Gothic and Renaissance

1457–1515   Venice. S. Zaccaria; façade
1481   „   Palazzo Vendramin
1490   „   Ducal Palace; inner court

To this list of buildings may be added, as an example of a typical fortified Italian hill-town, the beautiful little town of San Gimignano (S. Gimignano dalle belle torri), near Siena, which still possesses thirteen 12th–13th-century towers of an original alleged total of 72 (of which 25 were standing in 1580). The two famous private fortress-towers in Bologna are rather earlier (12th century), the Torre Asinelli being 321 feet high and the Torre Gari-senda 161 feet. Both are leaning considerably, and both are rather hideous.

6

Early Renaissance
Architecture

c. 1420 – *c.* 1500

THE FRENCH WORD *renaissance* (*rinascimento* in Italian; sometimes clumsily anglicized as "renascence") means literally "rebirth," and is used to describe the revival of interest in the classical culture of Greece and Rome, in contradistinction to the clerical scholarship of the medieval Church. The Renaissance certainly started in Italy, but no precise date can be assigned to its beginning, and the movement had been in vogue for a long time before it had any noticeable effect upon architecture.

It began with a revival of classical literary scholarship (e.g. in the poems of Petrarch), and may also be detected as early as the 13th century in the work of various sculptors, especially Niccolò Pisano and his son Andrea, e.g. the tomb of S. Dominic at Bologna (1221), the pulpits of Pisa (1260) and Siena (1268) cathedrals; and in a fountain at Perugia, where the figure sculpture recalls that on late Roman sarcophagi. Classical influence also appears in some of the paintings of Giotto at a somewhat later date.

82

PLATE VII

Florence: Palazzo Medici-Riccardi, exterior (*Photo: Alinari*)

PLATE VIII

Rome: St. Peter's, showing dome and apse

Venice: The Loggetta (*Photo: Alinari*)

Other circumstances also favoured the movement: interest in the antiquities of Rome fostered by Martin V (Pope
from 1417 to 1431) in Rome, and by the powerful
Medici family of bankers in Florence; the importation to
Italy of antiquities from Byzantium, which fell to the
Turks in 1453; the discovery in 1414 of the forgotten MS.
by Vitruvius of his treatise on architecture (cf. p. 20)
and its subsequent publication; and the invention of the
printing-press, leading to the production of other books
on architecture, notably one by Alberti, which appeared
in 1485 after his death and was partly based upon
Vitruvius.

More important than any of these various factors, however, was the work of Filippo Brunelleschi (1377–1446), a
Florentine architect; and it may be observed that from
his time onwards the chief buildings of Italy are most
conveniently treated here under the names of their
designers; whereas previously in Italy—though less so
than in Northern countries—the identity of the architect
is too often unknown. The reasons for this anonymity—as
I have explained elsewhere[1]—are partly to be found in
the jealousy or indifference of the clerical scribes who
compiled the records of the medieval cathedrals and
abbeys, and were more concerned to honour the memory
and flatter the ego of the bishop, abbot or prior who had
ordered the church in question to be erected. *Fieri fecit*
is the usual phrase, meaning that "he ordered it to be
built," not that he designed it. This was perhaps natural,
because the scribe felt no urge whatever to perpetuate
the work of a man who—contrary to popular Victorian
belief—was a hired layman and an outsider, not a monk
or a priest. Biographies of all the chief Italian architects

[1] See my book *The Architect in History* (1927).

from Giotto onwards are included in the famous book *Le Vite de' piu eccellenti Architetti, Pittore e Scultori da Cimabue insino a tempi nostri* ("Lives of the most excellent Architects, Painters and Sculptors from Cimabue up to our own times") by Giorgio Vasari, a mediocre architect but an admirable historian. His great work, first published at Florence in 1551, has since been translated into the chief European languages (e.g. English, in *Everyman's Library*).

Brunelleschi's father intended him to become a lawyer, but "perceiving that the mind of the boy was constantly intent on various intricate questions of art and mechanics made him learn writing and arithmetic, and then placed him in the Guild of the Goldsmiths, that he might acquire design from a friend of his."[1] But Filippo had other ideas, and at about the age of 25 he set out with his young friend Donatello the sculptor to study the architecture of the ancient ruins of Rome. In order to obtain funds he sold a farm, and took up gem-setting in Rome as a means of livelihood. "And as Filippo was free from all household cares he gave himself up so exclusively to his studies that he took no time either to eat or sleep; his every thought was of architecture, which was then extinct: I mean the good old manner, and not the Gothic and barbarous one which was much practised at that period. . . . Filippo did this because . . . architecture is much more useful to men than either painting or sculpture."[1]

Brunelleschi had two objects in mind when he began his studies: firstly to revive the use of Roman architecture; and secondly to discover from the ruins some method of constructing a dome for the (new) Gothic cathedral of S. Maria del Fiore at Florence—a problem

[1] Vasari.

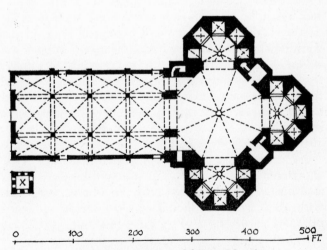

Cathedral of S. Maria del Fiore, Florence
X denotes "Giotto's Campanile"

which was then baffling all the architects of that city, and which he, at this early age, had thus determined to solve. So, with the one purpose in view, he and Donatello excavated and measured and drew so assiduously that the local populace suspected them of being treasure-hunters; while on the other hand Brunelleschi devoted special attention to examining ancient brick buildings, studying the principles of their vaulting and the methods by which bricks and stones were cramped together with metal fastenings. Meanwhile his long study of the ruins had the result that "he became capable of entirely reconstructing the city in his imagination, and of beholding Rome as she had been before she was ruined."[1]

Returning to Florence in 1407 he was successful in the competition for the cathedral dome, but the work was not carried out till 1419; and the crowning lantern—for which he left a wooden model (now worm-eaten, but still to be seen in the museum of the Opera del Duomo adjoining the cathedral)—was not finished until after his death. His dome itself is slightly pointed in form, and consists of inner and outer shells (like that of St Peter's at Rome, p. 110). It rises from an octagonal base, 138 feet 6 inches in diameter; and its design is a most successful compromise between Renaissance and Gothic architecture, for ribs carry the main weight, in the Gothic manner of vaulting.

Brunelleschi's other buildings—all in or near Florence —are listed on p. 94. Of these the most important is the church of S. Spirito, one of his latest works. It is as large as a small cathedral, 325 feet long, and of cruciform plan, with aisles carried all round including transepts and chancel. Over the central nave is a flat ceiling, but the aisles are

[1] Vasari.

divided into square bays, each roofed with a dome in Byzantine fashion, while there is a large and low dome on pendentives over the crossing. The round arches of the nave-arcade do not spring directly from the capitals of the columns supporting them, but from a block serving the same purpose as a Byzantine pulvin, worked into the form of a classical entablature (see p. 19 illustrating the Orders of architecture). This curious treatment, found occasionally in late Roman work, is illogical and rather unsightly, showing that in spite of Brunelleschi's great originality and good taste he was still somewhat pedantic-ally bound by the rules of Vitruvius and "the ancients." The same device was adopted by Wren, more than two centuries later, and by Gibbs for certain of their London churches; but Brunelleschi did not use it in the portico of his church for the Spedale degli Innocenti (Foundling Hospital), also at Florence, where the arches spring direct from the capital. This delightful and well-known build-ing is decorated with circular plaques of children in swaddling-clothes, executed in glazed blue and white earthenware by Andrea della Robbia, who also provided a beautiful lunette of the Annunciation in the same material. The church of the Badia (= abbey) at Fiesole near Florence, designed by Brunelleschi but completed after his death, is also cruciform. Except that these charming buildings have one defect (in the apparent slenderness of the arcade-columns carrying a rather heavy load of wall above them), his work is invariably delicate and refined—more so, indeed, than most of the Roman models upon which he relied—and very original.

The enormous palace that he designed for Luca Pitti, chief magistrate of the Florentine Republic, is one of the

G

largest in Italy, with the colossal frontage of 475 feet and a height of 114 feet. Brunelleschi began building it in 1435, but it was not finished until a century later, long after his death; and, as we now see it, only the lower storeys of the central block are his work. It is a pompous house for a rich man, whom we should now call a profiteer, and looks it! Ruskin, in a charitable and poetical moment, wrote that it is "brother heart to the mountain from which it is rent"; and indeed it set a fashion in Florence for cyclopean masonry on the exterior of plutocrats' palaces. Its plan is magnificent, grouped around three internal courts and a huge open forecourt. It certainly proclaims the arrival of the Renaissance of Roman architecture.

The other leading exponent of the movement in Florence was Michelozzo Michelozzi (1396–1472), several years younger than Brunelleschi, from whom he evidently derived most of his ideas. Like him Michelozzo started as a worker in other crafts, and did not turn to architecture until he was 40; but he left his mark on Florence, on many other Italian cities and even so far afield as Ragusa (now Dubrovnik) across the Adriatic. In Florence he remodelled the convent and church of S. Marco; but his greatest work was the huge Palazzo Riccardi (properly "Medici-Riccardi"), which he built for Cosimo de' Medici, the banker, who had become, it was said, the richest man in Europe. Here again everything about the building suggests a rich man's house, crowned by a colossal stone cornice above its walls of massive stone blocks. It looks as if it could resist a siege by the populace or by an invader; and, though there was nothing like it in ancient Rome, it looks truly Roman. Vasari relates that Cosimo consulted Brunelleschi in the first instance, but concluded that the design prepared for him by the latter

was too sumptuous and magnificent . . . and because it would have excited envy among the citizens which would more than counterbalance the gain to the city by its beauty and convenience or the advantage to himself. Accordingly the one designed by Michelozzo pleased him, and he caused it to be completed in its present form so conveniently and with so much beauty that there are majesty and grandeur in its very simplicity. Michelozzo deserves the more praise because this building was the first to be erected after the modern order, containing a useful and beautiful division into apartments.

The Strozzi Palace in Florence (1489–1553), by Benedetto da Majano, closely follows the design of the Palazzo Riccardi; and its huge stone cornice overhangs the street, far below, by more than 7 feet. It is a solemn thought that these great Italian town houses of nearly 500 years ago have provided the models for half the clubs in London, and for other structures in Manchester, Bradford and even New York.

The Early Renaissance in Rome is much less important than in Florence. Alberti, the scholar-architect (p. 83), worked there on the church of S. Marco (1455–68) and the adjoining Venetian palace (Palazzo Venezia as it is now called in Italian), and Pontelli on some buildings listed on p. 95; but the outstanding architect of the period was Donato Bramante of Urbino (1444–1514), whose real surname was Lazzaro. He started his career as a painter, turned to architecture while living in Milan and settled permanently in Rome in 1499. There he had already designed the cloister of S. Maria della Pace (1494) and probably the Palazzo della Cancelleria (1495–1511). Meanwhile he had begun an important commission for

the Pope—the remodelling of the Vatican Palace, starting
with the Belvedere Court in 1484–92. This was followed
by his greatest work, his design for the new cathedral of
St Peter, a year before the actual construction began in
1506. Because his buildings were mainly erected in the
early years of the 16th century they are described in the

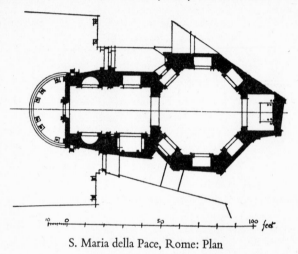

S. Maria della Pace, Rome: Plan

next chapter, which deals with the "Middle Renaissance"
from *c.* 1500 to *c.* 1550, and contains some comment on
Bramante's work as a whole. His numerous buildings in
Lombardy and Milan are listed on p. 96, and it has been
said of them that they have "the free natural character of
the golden age" of the Renaissance, i.e. before the rules
of Vitruvius, Palladio and Vignola had begun to domin-
ate architectural design, as explained later in this book.
Bramante is also credited with the design of the church of
S. Bernardino (1475) in his native town of Urbino.

Turning now to Venetia, we find that—with the sole exception of the Palazzo del Consiglio at Verona (1476), by the monkish architect Fra Giocondo, a pleasant building with an arcaded lower storey—all the examples of Renaissance architecture earlier than 1500 are in Venice (see list on p. 96), and all, so far as is known, are the work

Arabesque in marble: Church of S. Maria dei Miracoli, Venice (1480)

of the Lombardi family of architects and their disciples. The church of S. Maria dei Miracoli at Venice (1480–9), by Pietro Lombardo, seems to have been inspired by the older cathedral of St Mark (p. 66), both in the design of its dome and in the fact that it is inlaid with coloured marbles, like that famous Byzantine masterpiece. It is full of beautiful ornamental detail and delicate arabesques carved in marble, but it is a simple little building without aisles or transepts.

The Palazzo Dario (1450) on the Grand Canal, by the Lombardi family, shows an equally skilful and attractive use of coloured marbles; and the façade of the Scuola di S. Marco (1485) is also in the same style of the Lombardi, displaying much delicate ornament. Of the other palaces lining the Grand Canal, the Palazzo Cornaro Spinelli (1481), by Pietro Lombardo, has a classical cornice, and the lowest storey has "rusticated" (i.e. rough) blocks of masonry—an idea possibly borrowed from the older Riccardi Palace at Florence; but the windows of the two upper storeys, though round-headed, are divided by central shafts into smaller arches with something like Gothic tracery above.

The Palazzo Vendramin, also built by Pietro Lombardo in 1481, is more classical in style, with strongly marked cornices dividing its façades into three storeys, and a very bold crowning cornice. The "orders" are freely introduced on its handsome façade to the Grand Canal.

The inner courtyard of the Doge's or Ducal Palace (1486 onwards), by A. Rizzo, is much more classical and less Gothic in style than the two fronts to the Grand Canal and the Piazzetta, already mentioned (p. 78). The quaint Torre dell' Orologio (clock-tower), adjoining St Mark's, was erected c. 1494-6.

In Lombardy this early phase of the Renaissance is represented by the Ospedale Maggiore at Milan, designed by Antonio Filarete in 1547, a fine building in terracotta; the church of S. Maria at Brescia, by L. Beretta (1487); and the façade (1491) added by Borgognone, Solari and others to the much more ornate and rather older Certosa at Pavia; also by the buildings designed by Bramante before he left Milan for Rome (see p. 96).

In Bologna, and in the part of Italy between Tuscany on the south and Lombardy on the north, there are several notable buildings of the Early Renaissance, before 1500 (see list on p. 95). Of these the most important are the churches of S. Francesco at Rimini (1446), and of S. Sebastiano (1460) and S. Andrea (1472–1512), both at Mantua—all designed by Leone Battista Alberti (1404–1472) who has already been mentioned as the author of a book on architecture. He was trained as a lawyer, and indeed obtained a doctorate in law at the university of Bologna, not turning to architecture until he had also dabbled in poetry and philosophy. His importance in the story of Italian architecture is due to his status as a versatile pioneer of the Renaissance movement, especially in his remodelling of S. Andrea at Rimini, a cruciform church to which he added a rather bleak and very classical façade, with a deep and lofty central portal flanked by flat Corinthian pilasters—a truly Roman design, but never completed. It came to be known as the "Tempio Malatestiana," after the bloodthirsty tyrant, Sigismondo Malatesta, who commissioned it; but its unfinished state tends to blind one's eyes to the excellence of many features of its design; while the interior suggests the danger of attempting to make the best of both worlds—Renaissance and Gothic.

The city of Genoa, though famous in Italian history long before 1500, received the impact of the Renaissance movement very late, and has nothing significant to show of the early phase of Renaissance architecture except a series of really beautiful marble doorways, framed with graceful arabesque bands, and with panels carved with sculpture in low relief over their openings.

In southern Italy and Sicily, too, there is a scarcity of

notable Renaissance buildings right up to the time when the Baroque movement made its sensational appearance there in the 17th century. Even the city of Naples has only two examples worth mention: a couple of monumental gateways, the Arch of Alfonso (1470) and the Porta Capuana (1484), designed by the Milanese Pietro di Martino and by the Florentine Giuliano da Majano respectively.

EARLY RENAISSANCE BUILDINGS
(c. 1420–c. 1500)

Florence, Tuscany, Umbria

1419–61	Florence.	Dome of cathedral	Brunelleschi
1421–44	,,	Spedale degli Innocenti	,,
1424	,,	S. Lorenzo, old sacristy	,,
1430–46	,,	Cappella dei Pazzi	,,
1433 on	,,	S. Spirito	,,
1435 on	,,	S. Croce, 2nd cloister	,,
,,	,,	Palazzo Pitti	,,
1442	,,	Palazzo Quaratesi	,,
c. 1437–52	,,	Monastery of S. Marco	Michelozzo
c. 1444–59	,,	Palazzo Medici-Riccardi	,,
c. 1445	,,	SS. Annunziata	,,
1451	,,	Palazzo Rucellai	Alberti
1454	,,	Palazzo Vecchio, *cortile*	Michelozzo
1456	,,	S. Maria Novella, façade	Alberti
1460	Siena.	Loggia del Papa	Federighi
,,	,,	Palazzo del Diavolo	,,
1462	Fiesole.	Badia	Brunelleschi
1463	Siena.	Palazzo Nerucci	Rossellino
1472	Todi.	S.M. della Consolazione	Bramante
1480	Florence.	Palazzo Antinori	
		? G. da Sangallo or B. d'Agnolo	
1489–1553	,,	Palazzo Strozzi	
		B. da Majano & Cronaca	

| 1490 | Florence. Palazzo Gondi | G. da Sangallo |
| 1495 | ,,   Palazzo Vecchio, Great Hall | Cronaca |

Of buildings listed above, S. Spirito and the Palazzo Pitti were damaged in the Second World War.

Rome

1455-7	Palazzo Venezia (formerly S. Marco)	
		Alberti or G. da Majano
1468	S. Marco, church of	,,
1473-81	Vatican Palace: Sistine Chapel	G. de' Dolci
,,	Spedale di S. Spirito	Pontelli
1477	S. Maria del Popolo	,,
1484	Vatican Palace: Cortile del Belvedere	Bramante
,,	S.M. della Pace (but façade later)	Pontelli
1494-1504	,, cloister	Bramante
1495-1511	Palazzo della Cancelleria	,, (?)
,,	S. Lorenzo in Damaso	,, (?)
1495	S. Trinità dei Monti	?
1496-1504	Palazzo Torlonia, formerly Giraud Montecavallo	

(For later work by Bramante, see list on pp. 106-7)

Bologna, The Marches, etc.

1446	Rimini. S. Francesco	Alberti
1460	Mantua. S. Sebastiano	,,
1467-82	Urbino. Palazzo Ducale	Laurana & Pontelli
1472-1512	Mantua. S. Andrea	Alberti
1474-1513	Faenza. Cathedral	G. da Majano
1475	Urbino. S. Bernardino	Bramante
1484-92	Bologna. Palazzo Bevilacqua-Vincenzi	Nardi
1492-1567	Ferrara. Palazzo dei Diamanti	B. Rossetti
1496	,, S. Francesco	,,
1498-1553	,, S. Cristoforo	(?) Sansovino

Of buildings listed above, the Palazzo dei Diamanti and S. Cristoforo, both at Ferrara, were slightly damaged in the Second World War.

Lombardy and Piedmont

1452–76	Milan. Castello Sforzesco, rebuilding of	A. Filarete
1457	„ Ospedale Maggiore	„
1474	„ S. Maria presso S. Satiro	? Bramante
1477	Abbiategrasso. Entrance court to church	Bramante
1479	Milan. S. Satiro, sacristy	„
1486	Como Cathedral, eastern portion	T. Rodari
1487	Brescia. S. Maria dei Miracoli	L. Beretta
1490	Milan. S. Maria presso S. Celso	Bramante
1491 on	Pavia. The Certosa, façade	Borgognone or Solari
1492	Milan. S. Maria delle Grazie, eastern part	Bramante
„	„ S. Ambrogio, cloister	„
„	Brescia. Palazzo del Municipio ("La Loggia")	? Bramante (followed by others)

Of buildings listed above, the Ospedale Maggiore, S.M. delle Grazie and S. Ambrogio—all at Milan—and S.M. dei Miracoli at Brescia were severely damaged in the Second World War.

Venice and Venetia

1450	Venice. Palazzo Dario	School of the Lombardi
1476	Verona. Palazzo del Consiglio	Giocondo
1480–9	Venice. S. Maria dei Miracoli	P. Lombardo
1481	„ Palazzo Cornaro-Spinelli	School of the Lombardi
„	„ Palazzo Vendramin	P. Lombardo
1485	„ Scuola di S. Marco	M. Lombardo
c. 1485	„ Palazzo Trevisano	?
1496	„ Torre del Orologio	P. Lombardo
1499	„ Ducal Palace, *cortile*	A. Rizzo

None of these buildings appears to have been damaged in the Second World War.

7

Middle Renaissance Architecture

c. 1500 – c. 1550

THE DATES given above as the limits of this chapter are admittedly arbitrary, and are used as a matter of convenience. It was about 1500 (1499 to be precise) that Bramante finally settled in Rome, and only a few years later that he was appointed, on the recommendation of Michelangelo according to tradition, to prepare plans for the complete rebuilding of St Peter's. This half-century of Roman architecture has been called the "High Renaissance," and is most closely associated with the names of four great architects—Bramante, Antonio Sangallo, Jacopo Sansovino and Peruzzi—who were primarily if not solely architects; and with another, Raphael, who is better known as a painter. Michelangelo, a master of all three arts—architecture, sculpture and painting—joined the list midway in the period; but Vignola, its leading figure, did not settle in Rome until near its end (in 1546), so his work is more appropriately discussed in my next chapter. The term High Renaissance, now commonly applied by scholars to the later work of Bramante and some of his contemporaries, seems to imply the culmination of the Renaissance in Italian architecture, before it came to be consciously and artificially bound to a style or "manner" prescribed by academic tradition and regulated by rules formulated in textbooks: hence the term Mannerism, used since *c.* 1920 to cover the period between the "High Renaissance" and the beginning of the Baroque period, *c.* 1600. There are exceptions, however, to any such classification.

Generally speaking, the centre of gravity in Italian architecture had passed from Florence to Rome about the year 1500, and was very largely connected with the power of the Papacy in Rome. During the 16th–17th centuries, besides the great reconstruction schemes at St Peter's and the Vatican Palace, there was a tremendous boom in church-building in Rome; and among many fine town houses in the city and handsome villas on its outskirts the majority were erected by prominent papal families. Three of the leading popes in the 16th century—Leo X (1513–21), Clement VII (1523–34) and Pius IV (1559–65) —belonged to the famous Florentine family of Medici; and others whose names are connected with palace-building came from the families of Farnese, Ghislieri, Boncompagni and Aldobrandini. In the 17th century, where the name of Medici appears yet again, we find also Borghese, Ludovisi, Barberini, Pamfili, Chigi, Rospigliosi and Altieri— every one of them the builder of some magnificent palace or villa in or near Rome. Everywhere one sees their heraldic emblem carved or painted—e.g. the Barberini bee and the Farnese fleur-de-lis—just as in the contemporary châteaux of Touraine one constantly encounters the badges of François I and of his mistress Diane de Poitiers.

Yet this was a very disturbed period in Italy, ecclesias-
tically and politically. The schism between the popes of
Rome and the anti-popes of Avignon had been healed
long before 1500, but the Reformation was now in full
swing; and was answered by the Counter-Reformation,
centred in Rome and leading to the founding of the
Society of Jesus (the Jesuits) in 1540 and of the Oratorians

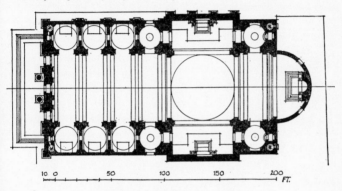

The Gesù Church, Rome: Plan

in 1556. The consequential effects of these movements in
Italy, and especially in Rome, upon the quantity and the
quality of church architecture were enormous.

Politically great damage ensued from the Sack of Rome
in 1527, when an invading army of "forty thousand half-
starved savages" under the Duke of Bourbon came to
the rescue of the noble Colonna family, one of whose
number, a cardinal, was at loggerheads with the Pope,
Clement VII. It was really a quarrel between the Pope and
the French on the one hand and the Colonna family
backed by the (Holy) Roman Emperor on the other.

Under Pope Leo X (1513–21) the population of the

city had been about 90,000; after the Sack of Rome
(1527) it dropped to about 30,000, but then rose again
during the pontificate of Sixtus V (1585–90) from about
45,000 to about 100,000. These bald figures show to what
a low level Rome sank after 1527, and how miraculously
it recovered. (It may be recalled that its population is
estimated to have varied between $1\frac{1}{4}$ and $1\frac{1}{2}$ million in
the 2nd century A.D., and to have sunk to about 17,000
while the popes were at Avignon, 1309–77. By way of
comparison it was about 500,000 in 1907 and is now
approaching 2,000,000.)

Returning now to Bramante and his buildings erected
in Rome during the first decade of the 16th century, we
find that critics are at variance about his Palazzo della
Cancelleria (i.e. Chancery) near the Vatican, built some
time between 1483 and 1511. Certainly it shows nothing
of the "light-hearted . . . Early Renaissance way" (to
quote one critic) of his buildings at Milan in his first
period. It has been suggested that his originality was
atrophied by contact with Leonardo da Vinci at Milan;
but, at any rate to the mind of the present writer, the
Cancelleria externally is the dullest and most uninspired
building of Renaissance Rome, with its three nearly
equal storeys, its over-rusticated masonry and its general
dreariness. The Palazzo Giraud (now Torlonia), 1496–
1504, designed by A. Montecavallo, is said to have
been copied from it, and certainly repeats most of its
defects.

In 1502 Bramante designed what most people regard as
his best building: the so-called "Tempietto" (= little
temple) erected in the courtyard of the older church of
S. Pietro in Montorio, as a shrine to mark the traditional
spot where St Peter was crucified. It is a lovely little

circular building, with an austere Roman Doric colonnade, and suggests a Greek *tholos* rather than any antique
Roman building. "Montorio," by the way, is derived
from Latin Mons Aureus, the golden hill, referring to the
sandy hill—the Janiculum—on which it stands.

Another very small building, the chapel or oratory of
S. Giovanni in Oleo (1509), close to the Porta Latina in
the walls of Rome, is attributed to Bramante, but its
interior was altered later by Borromini.

In 1503 Bramante began remodelling the Vatican
Palace for the Pope. His first work was the Cortile di S.
Damaso; and soon afterwards he was commissioned to
design a new cathedral to replace the old basilica of St
Peter's, first built by order of Constantine the Great in
324–49 on the site of St Peter's tomb adjoining the Circus
of Nero (cf. p. 42). It had already become ruinous in 1452
when Pope Nicholas V started its restoration; but Julius
II, in or shortly before 1506, instructed Bramante to
demolish it entirely. This he did so thoroughly that his
contemporaries (and jealous rivals) humorously or
enviously nicknamed him "Maestro Ruinante."

Bramante's design took the form of a Greek cross (with
four equal arms, not a Latin cross with a long nave); but
just as Wren furnished a Greek-cross design for St Paul's
in London 160 years later which was rejected for ritual
reasons advanced by the clergy, so Bramante's design
was altered to a Latin-cross plan (after his death in 1514)
by his successor Raphael, who, it may be recalled, practised architecture while still continuing to paint Madon-
nas.

As ultimately built, and as we now see it, the main
bulk of the cathedral is a combination of Bramante's
plan and Raphael's, made by Baldassare Peruzzi (p. 103),

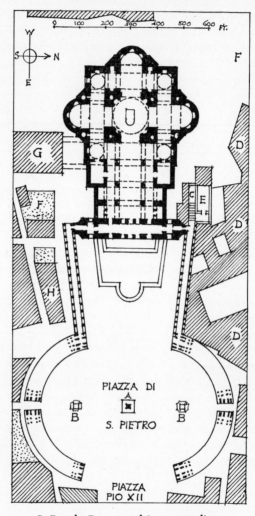

St Peter's, Rome, and its surroundings

A, Obelisk; B, Fountains; C, Scala Regia;
D, Vatican Palace; E, Sistine Chapel;
F, Gardens; G, Sacristy; H, Museum.

who succeeded to the charge of the work in 1520. He was followed, at his death in 1536, by Giuliano da Sangallo, and he in turn by Michelangelo in 1546 when the latter was 71 years of age. Then came Giacomo della Porta and Domenico Fontana in 1588, who finished Michelangelo's dome; Maderno in 1606–12, who spoilt the general effect by extending the length of the nave and adding the pompous façade, and finally Bernini, whose noble colonnade and piazza (p. 126) deserve nothing but praise. Thus this gigantic building, with its great merits and its numerous defects, is the composite product of a succession of able architects over a period of 170 years; and further description of it will appear in the next two chapters.

Baldassare Peruzzi (1481–1536) was born near Siena in Tuscany, where his earliest work—as a painter—was done before he came to Rome, where he designed the beautiful Villa Farnesina (1506–11), the Palazzo Lante (1520), the Palazzo Ossoli (c. 1520), the Palazzi Massimi alle Colonne and Angelo Massimi (1529), and a palace in the Valle Giulia (1530). Outside Rome his work included the Palazzo Albergati (1521–40) and the church of S. Michele in Bosco (1523)—both at Bologna. His work is invariably scholarly and excellent, showing an almost Greek sense of refinement; and his town houses—many of them on cramped sites—are planned with great ingenuity and good taste.

Antonio da Sangallo the Younger (1483–1546), another famous architect of this period, born in Florence, was the nephew of an architect of the same name and of Giuliano da Sangallo. Journeying to Rome as a youth to study the classical buildings there, he met and was encouraged by Bramante. After taking a hand with the designs for St Peter's he designed on his own

H

account S. Maria di Loreto (1507) and the Farnese Palace (begun in 1513) in Rome; completed the Villa Madama, Rome, which Raphael had left unfinished; and also planned the fortifications of Civitavecchia and some other towns.

Raphael—as he is commonly called in English today—is more correctly known as Raffaello Sanzio (or Santi) of Urbino, where he was born in 1483. Starting, like some other architects already mentioned, as a painter, he had already attained some reputation when, in 1508, he was summoned to Rome to execute the famous series of large paintings in the Stanze (State Apartments) of the Vatican. Six years later, apparently without any training whatever as an architect, he was given complete charge of the re-building of St Peter's, as previously explained. In 1509, however, he had designed the small chapel or oratory of S. Eligio degli Orefici, near the river and not far from the Colosseum. His other architectural work in or near the city comprises the Villa Madama (1516), now somewhat decayed, on the wooded slopes of Monte Mario near Rome; and the façade of the Palazzo Vidoni-Caffarelli (1515 or 1520) towards the Via del Sudario, next door to S. Andrea della Valle. The Palazzo Spada, near the Palazzo Farnese, is also attributed to him, and looks like a painter's architecture, but was not finished till 1540, long after his death.

Jacopo Sansovino (1486–1570), who worked in Rome from 1505 to 1527, was a Florentine citizen. His real surname was Tatti; but he afterwards adopted the surname of his master, Antonio Sansovino (called Contucci), who started as a sculptor, executed several fine tombs in Venice and elsewhere and also carried out some architectural work at the Casa Santa (= Holy House) at Loreto. Jacopo studied in Rome, and built the church of S. Marcello (1519), but fled from the city when it was sacked in 1527. He became architect to the Republic of Venice in 1529, in that capacity designing a number of fine buildings in Venice which are listed on p. 107.

The same list names a palace in Venice by Michele Sanmicheli (1484–1559), born in Verona of a distinguished family of architects. After studying in Rome he was engaged from 1520 onwards in remodelling the fortifications of his native city, including the fine Porta Nuova (1535) and the Porta Palio (1524–57). These buildings, utilitarian in purpose, are of the highest architectural merit—massive and dignified. They may be compared with English examples: the fort at Tilbury in Essex (1682) and the rather Baroque Citadel Gate at Plymouth (1670); also with the handsome Rheintor at Breisach on the Rhine, designed by the great military engineer Vauban in 1703. The last was certainly, the others were possibly, inspired by Sanmicheli. That gifted architect's other works included at least half a dozen palaces in Verona, also fortifications for the Venetian Republic on the Lido of Venice, at Brescia, Bergamo, Legnano and Peschiera, and in Dalmatia and Crete.

The Middle or High Renaissance period produced no buildings of note in southern Italy or Sicily; and in Genoa only the Palazzo Andrea Doria (1529) by Montorsoli, which suffered damage in the Second World War.

MIDDLE RENAISSANCE BUILDINGS
(c. 1500–c. 1550)

Florence, Tuscany, Umbria

1504	Florence. S. Salvatore del Monte	Cronaca
1516	„ Palazzo Pandolfini	
		Raphael, then G. Sangallo
1518	Montepulciano. S. Maria di S. Biagio	
		A. Sangallo
1520	Florence. Palazzo Bartolini	B. d'Agnolo
1523–9	„ S. Lorenzo, new sacristy	
		Michelangelo
1524	„ Laurentian Library	„
1540	„ Palazzo Torregiani	B. d'Agnolo
1547–9	Caprarola. Castle (see p. 112)	Vignola

Bologna, The Marches, etc.

1508	Ferrara. Palazzo Roverella	—
1509	Loreto. Casa Santa Bramante, A. Sansovino, etc.	
1510	„ Palazzo Apostolico	Bramante
1512 on	Civitavecchia, fortifications of	
		Bramante, Michelangelo
1520–40	Mantua. Palazzo Ducale	G. Romano
1521	Bologna. Palazzo Albergati	Peruzzi
1523	„ S. Michele in Bosco	„
1525–35	Mantua. Palazzo del Tè	G. Romano
1530	„ Palazzo di Giustizia	„

Venice and Venetia

1504 on	Venice. Palazzo Contarini delle Figure	
		Style of the Lombardi
1506	„ Fondaco de' Tedeschi	G. Tedesco
1514	„ S. Zaccaria, façade of	M. Lombardo
1516–32	Padua. S. Giustina	Riccio

1517–47	Venice. Scuola di S. Rocco	
		P. Lombardo & Scarpagnino
1524	Verona. Porta Palio	Sanmicheli
1530	„ Palazzo Bevilacqua	„
c. 1530	„ Palazzo Canossa	„
„	„ Palazzo Pompei	„
1535	„ Porta Nuova	„
1536	Venice. Libreria Vecchia	J. Sansovino
„	„ La Zecca (the Mint)	„
1538	„ S. Giorgio dei Greci	„
1538–77	„ Doge's Palace: Scala d'Oro	„
1540	„ Loggetta near Campanile	„
„	„ S. Martino	„
1548	„ Palazzo Corner-Mocenigo	Sanmicheli
1549–56	„ Palazzo Grimani	„

Genoa

| 1529 | Genoa. Palazzo Andrea Doria | Montorsoli |

Rome

c. 1483–1511	Palazzo della Cancelleria	Bramante
1500	S. Maria del Anima	Bramante & Peruzzi
„	S. Pietro in Montorio	Pontelli
1502–10	„	"Tempietto." Bramante
1496–1504	Palazzo Giraud, later Torlonia	A. Montecavallo
c. 1503	Vatican Palace, Cortile di S. Damaso	Bramante
1505	Palazzo Sora	„
1506	Villa Farnesina	Peruzzi
„	St Peter's, rebuilding began	Bramante
1507	S. Maria di Loreto	A. Sangallo
1509	S. Giovanni in Oleo	Bramante
„	S. Eligio degli Orefici	Raphael
„	Palazzo Orsini	Peruzzi
1513–50	Palazzo Farnese	A. Sangallo
1516	Villa Madama	Raphael, etc.

1519	S. Marcello (façade later)	Jac. Sansovino
1520	Palazzo Lante	Peruzzi
1529	Palazzi Massimi (two)	,,
1540	Villa Medici (inner façade later)	—
,,	Palazzo Spada	G. Mazzoni
1540–6	Palaces (two) on the Capitol	Michelangelo[1]
1546 on	Work at St Peter's	,, [1]
1549	Villa d'Este at Tivoli	Pirro Ligorio

Of the buildings listed here, the Casa Santa at Loreto and the Palazzo Ducale at Mantua were damaged in the Second World War; and the fortress of Civitavecchia seriously damaged.

[1] The work of Michelangelo is dealt with briefly in Chapter VIII.

8

Late Renaissance
or Mannerist Architecture

c. 1550 - *c.* 1600

As STATED in the previous chapter, Rome replaced
Florence as the most important centre of Italian architecture at the beginning of the 16th century, and retained
that pre-eminence until the year 1700 at least, in spite of
great activity in Venice and southern Italy during the
Baroque period of the 17th century. The fifty years or so
with which the present chapter is concerned were generally described as "Late Renaissance" up to about 1920,
when the new term "Mannerism" was coined to describe
most of the Italian architecture of the period, in which the
leading exponents of architectural design were Michelangelo, Vignola, Domenico Fontana, Ammannati and
Giacomo della Porta in Rome; Alessi in Genoa; Tibaldi
in Lombardy; Palladio and Scamozzi in Venetia. It is
perhaps significant that three of these nine men—Vignola,
Palladio and Scamozzi—wrote manuals of architectural
design based upon the classical "orders" formulated by
Vitruvius, just as Alberti had done in the previous

generation. The new term "Mannerism" seems to be intended to contrast the work of these nine men and their contemporaries with the more spontaneous and free style practised by Bramante, Raphael and the leaders of the Middle or High Renaissance. On the other hand no single title, "Mannerism" or any other, really describes all the range of buildings—some very dull, others very striking and bold—produced in Italy during these fifty years.

The Baroque phase which followed at the beginning of the next century was frankly a revolt against academic rigidity, as we shall see; and some critics have traced its genesis to certain features of Michelangelo's work, arguing, with a measure of plausibility, that a man who had been working all his life at notably bold painting and sculpture would inevitably carry a marked preference for the picturesque into architecture when he started its practice at 70 years of age. His experience was in fact just the sort that would encourage him to break all the rules laid down by the pedants. So the argument goes, and his few buildings were very important; when he became chief architect to St Peter's in 1546 he had already designed the magnificent group on the Capitol in Rome, and had converted the ruins of Diocletian's Baths into the noble church of S. Maria degli Angeli. It is said that he had wished to turn his terrific energy into architectural channels at a much earlier date; but that Bramante had cunningly persuaded the Pope to give the older man the commission for painting the ceiling of the Sistine Chapel, which would keep him busy with his paint-brush for years and thus prevent him from meddling with his architectural colleagues and subordinates. Be that as it may, Michelangelo, at 71 years of age, designed a better dome than either of his predecessors had done; and though it was still unfinished at his death, the drum on which it rests was completed. Moreover he left drawings and a model for its completion, which was carried out by Della Porta and finished by 1605. He also replanned the apsidal chapels on a grand scale. To appreciate the splendour of his achievement a visitor should obtain a ticket of admission to the Vatican Gardens, whence one can look down upon the towering apsidal end with its gigantic

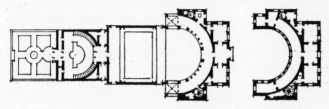

Villa di Papa Giulio, Rome: now Museo di Villa Giulia
Left: ground plan of Villa and its garden.
Right: plan of upper floor.

order of pilasters; for the familiar view of the cathedral from the Piazza gives no such impression of dignity, because the lengthening of the nave at a later date destroyed the original effect which depended upon the Greek-cross plan of the first design by Bramante.

Giacomo Barozzi da Vignola, commonly called Vignola after the place of his birth near Modena, was another great architect of this period. Starting his career as a painter, he studied architecture in Rome under Antonio Sangallo the Younger for some years, then worked in France for François I, and, after a short stay in Bologna, settled in Rome in 1546. There he designed the beautiful Villa Giulia or Palazzo di Papa Giulio, the Palace of Pope Julius III (1550-5), which stands nearly opposite the

British School at Rome and now houses the National Museum of Antiquities of Rome and the province of Lazio (Latium), admirably displayed in ideal surroundings. His other work includes two small churches in Rome and the great pentagonal palace or "castle" at Caprarola (1547–59), built for Cardinal Farnese. Moreover he designed the Gesù (Jesuit church) in Rome, which, begun in 1568, had a pronounced influence upon church-planning all over Europe during the long Baroque period of the 17th century. It has no aisles (their place being taken by a range of domed chapels on either side of the nave) but has shallow transepts, a shallow chancel with an apsidal end, and a dome over the "crossing." Vignola also wrote two books—one on the "five orders" of architecture (1562) and another on perspective, both of which have been translated into many languages. Yet most critics would agree that there is nothing pedantic about his buildings, which are original in plan and most successful in their method of lighting—a welcome change from medieval gloom. At Assisi Vignola designed the fine church of S. Maria degli Angeli (1559).

In Venetia during the same period the outstanding architect was Andrea Palladio (1518–80), whose influence upon English architecture from the time of Inigo Jones to that of Sir William Chambers was profound; and has made his native city of Vicenza, where his most important buildings were erected, a place of pilgrimage for architects ever since his day. From 1540 to 1550 he made an intensive study of the ancient buildings of Rome; and in 1570 published a manual, *I Quattro Libri dell' Architettura* ("The Four Books of Architecture"), which was soon translated into other tongues and became a classic. His chief buildings in Venice and Venetia are listed on p. 118. They are somewhat heavier and more academic in style than those of Vignola. The Banqueting House (now the United Services Museum) in Whitehall, London, designed by his admirer Inigo Jones and built in 1619–22, is a good example of the "Palladian" style, but there are many others in England.

In Venice Palladio's mantle fell upon Vincenzo Scamozzi (1552–1616), also a native of Vicenza, who completed the older man's dignified but rather monotonous Procuratie Nuove (1584), a block of buildings which form the south side of St Mark's Piazza at Venice, and are probably seldom noticed by tourists sitting in cafés beneath the arcades. Scamozzi, too, produced a book, *L'Idea dell' Architettura Universale*, published in Italian in 1615, in English in 1669, and also in other languages.

Compared with these giants the other leading architects of the period in Rome—Domenico Fontana (1543–1607), Bartolommeo Ammannati (1511–92) and Giacomo della Porta (*c.* 1540–1602)—are of less note; and some of their work is very dull. Their principal buildings are listed on p. 117.

That most entertaining writer Giorgio Vasari (1511–1574), whose delightful *Lives of the Painters, Sculptors and Architects* (to give it its English title)[1] first appeared in 1550 and has continued to be read with pleasure ever since, practised as an architect as well as a painter, but has left hardly any building of note, the Palazzo degli Uffizi at Florence (1560, now a famous picture-gallery) being his chief work.

There are few noteworthy examples of the period 1550–60 in southern Italy, Sicily or Bologna, but many in Lombardy, Piedmont and Genoa (listed on p. 119),

[1] English edition in *Everyman's Library* (4 vols.).

some of them being of great excellence and interest. Of the architects concerned the most outstanding are Alessi and Tibaldi. Galeazzo Alessi (1512–72) was born at Perugia, studied for some years in Rome, where he became an admirer of Michelangelo's work, and then built a number of fine palaces and the great church of S. Maria in Carignano—all in Genoa; some charming villas in the neighbourhood of Genoa; and also the important Palazzo Marino (1555, later the Municipio) and the façade of S. Maria presso S. Celso—both of these in Milan. His work is original, graceful and refined, with a complete absence of pedantry.

Another able architect of the same type was Pellegrino Tibaldi (1527–96), whose buildings are to be seen mainly in Milan and Lombardy (see list on p. 119) but also include two palaces and a church at Bologna (p. 119). The work of both these men deserves a higher degree of recognition than it has sometimes received.

The art or science of town-planning, as the term is interpreted today, had been largely forgotten during the Middle Ages, right up to the 16th century, although Leonardo da Vinci included some memoranda on its theoretical aspects in his voluminous writings between 1483 and 1516. It was then revived in Rome itself on the grand scale by Pope Sixtus V, and it is to him that we owe one of its finest examples. Rome had sunk to a very low level from its size in late classical days (when its population, as already mentioned, is estimated to have numbered between $1\frac{1}{4}$ and $1\frac{1}{2}$ million) to a mere 17,000 during the period (1309–77) when the popes resided at Avignon. Some account of its medieval condition appears in the splendid prose of Gibbon's *Decline and Fall*. Three-quarters of the area enclosed by the ancient walls

PLATE IX

Rome: Villa Giulia, exterior (*Photo: Alinari*)

Assisi: S. Maria degli Angeli, interior (*Photo: Alinari*)

PLATE X

Rome: St. Peter's, exterior showing piazza, etc.
(*Photo: Compagnia Fotocelere*)

Rome: Fontana di Trevi (*Photo: Alinari*)

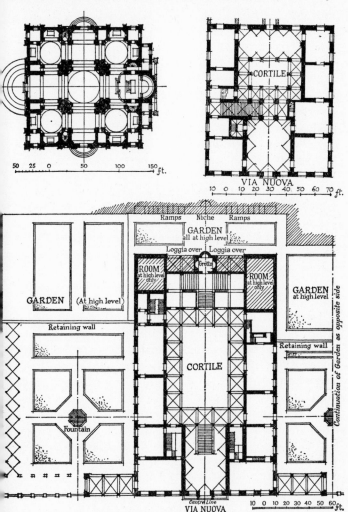

Late Renaissance Buildings in Genoa

Top left: S.M. in Carignano. Top right: Palazzo Cambiaso.
Below: Palazzo Doria-Tursi (now Municipio).

was occupied by gardens. Sheep grazed in the Forum Romanum and in the valley between the Palatine and Aventine hills. The people lived mostly in the lower quarters, where the numerous battlemented towers of the powerful nobles rose above crowded hovels and the neglected ruins of antiquity.

Pope Paul III (1447–64) began remodelling the city by straightening the Corso (the prolongation of the ancient Via Flaminia) from the church of S. Marco, at the foot of the Capitoline Hill, to the Arch of Marcus Aurelius, which was later replaced by the Porta del Popolo. In 1444–6 Flavio Biondo published a book, *Roma Instaurata*, which might be translated as "Rome Restored." Pope Sixtus IV (1471–84) caused a master plan of the city to be prepared, and built the Ponte Sisto across the Tiber in 1473. Alexander VI (1493–1503) replanned the Borgo on the east bank of the river; Julius II (1503–13) laid out the Via Giulia; and Leo X (1513–21) opened the Via Leonina, now the Via di Ripetta.

These civic improvements, interrupted by the Sack of Rome in 1527, were resumed under the next two popes; but even then the Coelian, Viminal and Quirinal hills still remained deserted. In 1540 Michelangelo planned the magnificent approach to the Capitol. Sixtus V (employing Domenico Fontana as his architect) proceeded in this work of replanning with great vigour. His major achievement was the creation of a series of streets converging on the famous pilgrimage-churches of S. Maria Maggiore and S. Giovanni in Laterano, comprising the present Vie Sistina, Felice, delle Quattro Fontane and di Porta S. Lorenzo. He also opened out the Lateran and Esquiline *piazze* and raised obelisks in four of the chief *piazze* of the city. During his rule the population—which had fallen from 90,000 to 30,000 after the Sack of Rome—rose again from 45,000 to 100,000. His schemes of town-planning were an unqualified success, and laid a sound basis for the additional splendours of the Baroque period which followed.

LATE RENAISSANCE OR MANNERIST BUILDINGS
(c. 1550–c. 1600)

Rome

1559 on	S. Maria degli Angeli	Michelangelo
1560	Casino del Papa, Vatican Gardens	P. Ligorio
1561	Porta del Popolo	Vignola, etc.
1568	Il Gesù	Vignola
1568–72	Palazzo dei Senatori (on Capitol)	
		Michelangelo & G. della Porta
1574	Palazzo del Quirinale, in part	D. Fontana, etc.
1576	University della Sapienza	G. della Porta
1582	Collegio Romano	B. Ammannati
1586	Palazzo del Laterano	D. Fontana
„	Palazzo Ruspoli	Ammannati
„	Palazzo Lancellotti	F. Volterra
1588	St Peter's, completion of dome	
		G. della Porta & D. Fontana
„	Vatican Library	D. Fontana
1589	S. Luigi dei Francesi	G. della Porta
1590	Palazzo Borghese	M. Longhi, senior
1591–1612	S. Andrea della Valle	Olivieri & Maderno

Naples

1584	S. Trinità Maggiore	—
1586	Museo Nazionale (previously a convent)	—
1590	S. Paolo Maggiore	Grimaldi
1592–1619	S. Filippo Neri	D. di Bartolommeo

Venice and Venetia

1549	Vicenza. Basilica	Palladio
1550	Padua. Cathedral A. della Valle & A. Righetto	
1551	Venice. S. Giorgio degli Schiavoni	
		J. Sansovino
1556	Vicenza. Palazzo Porto	Palladio
,,	,, Palazzo Valmarana	,,
1556–65	,, Palazzo Thiene	,,
1560	,, Palazzo Chiericati	,,
1560–75	Venice. S. Giorgio Maggiore	,,
1565	Maser. Villa Manin	,,
1565	Vicenza. Casa di Palladio	,,
1568	Venice. S. Francesco della Vigna, façade	,,
1570	Vicenza. Palazzo Barbarano	,,
,,	,, "Casa del Diavolo"	,,
1571	,, Palazzo Consiglio	,,
1576	Venice. Il Redentore	,,
1579	Vicenza. Teatro Olimpico Palladio & Scamozzi	
1584	Venice. Procuratie Nuove	Scamozzi
1588	Vicenza. Palazzo Trissino	,,
,,	Venice. Ponte Rialto	Antonio da Ponte
1589	,, Prison, façade to Grand Canal Contino	
1595–1605	,, Ponte dei Sospiri Antonio da Ponte	

Of the above buildings, the Basilica, the Palazzo Thiene, the Palazzo Valmarana and the Palazzo Trissino—all in Vicenza—were seriously damaged in the Second World War; and the cathedral at Padua was slightly damaged.

Bologna, The Marches, etc.

1558	Piacenza. Palazzo Farnese	Vignola
1562	Bologna. Portico di Banchi	,,
1570–86	Piacenza. S. Agostino	,,
1571–7	Loreto. Casa Santa, façade Boccalini & Venturi	
1575	Bologna. S. Pietro, choir of	Tibaldi
1576	,, Palazzo Magnani-Salem	,,

| 1577 | Bologna. Palazzo Arcivescovile | Tibaldi |
| 1587 | Ferrara. Palazzo dell' Università | G. Aleotti |

Florence, Umbria, etc.

1550–74	Florence. Palazzo degli Uffizi	Vasari
1566–9	„ Ponte S. Trinità	Ammannati
1568	„ Palazzo Pitti, in part	„
1569	Assisi. S. Maria degli Angeli	Vignola

Of the above buildings, the Ponte S. Trinità at Florence was destroyed in the Second World War, but has since been rebuilt.

Lombardy and Piedmont

1555	Milan. Palazzo Marino (now Municipio)	Alessi
c. 1558	Cernobbio. Villa d'Este (now a hotel)	—
1560	Milan. S. Vittore al Corpo	Alessi
„	„ Façade of cathedral	Tibaldi
1565	„ Arcivescovado	„
1569	„ S. Maria presso S. Celso, façade	Alessi
„	„ S. Fedele	Tibaldi
1580	Varese. S. Vittore (façade 1795)	„
1586	Gravedona. Palazzo del Pero	„

The Palazzo Marino at Milan was seriously damaged in the Second World War.

Genoa

1550	Palazzo Ducale	Pennone
„	Porta di Molo	Alessi
1552	Palazzo Spinola	„ ?
1552–1603	S. Maria in Carignano	„
1555–6	Palazzo Sauli	::
„	„ Marcello Durazzo	„
1556	„ Rosso or Brignole-Sale	„ ?
1560	„ Carega-Cataldi	G. B. Castello ?
„	„ Imperiale	„

I

1564	Palazzo Doria-Tursi (later Municipio)	
		R. Lurago
1565	„ Gambaro	G. Ponzello
„	„ Cambiaso	Alessi
1565 on	„ Pallavicini	F. Casella
1565–9	„ Bianco	D. & G. Ponzello
1567	Cathedral, dome	Alessi
1567–81	Palazzo Lercari-Parodi	„
1570–95	Borsa or Loggia dei Mercanti	F. Roderio
1579	S. Pietro dei Banchi	R. Lurago
c. 1587	S. Ambrogio	D. Ponzello
1587 on	SS. Annunziata (façade later)	G. della Porta

In the suburbs of Genoa

1548	Villa Cambiaso at S. Francesco d'Albaro	Alessi
c. 1560	Villa Scassi at Sampierdarena	„
1560–72	Villa Peschiere	„

The Ducale, Cambiaso, Spinola, and Doria-Tursi palaces were severely damaged in the Second World War; also the church of SS. Annunziata.

9

Baroque Architecture
in Rome

c. 1600 – *c.* 1750

ACCORDING TO the *Oxford Dictionary* the word Baroque was first used in English in 1818. Obviously it is not really English, but French; and its equivalents in German and Italian are *Barock* and *Barocco* respectively. It is derived from the Portuguese *barroco*, meaning a rough or mis-shapen pearl; and when applied to architecture it was used primarily as a nickname or term of abuse to describe a style of architecture which, a century ago at any rate, was considered to be odd, grotesque, bombastic, vulgar and altogether deserving of contempt.

It is perhaps significant that when James Fergusson published his widely read *Handbook of Architecture . . . of all Ages and all Countries* in 1859 he made no reference whatever to it in a thousand packed pages; but then he did not even mention Renaissance architecture—for him the whole story ended before 1500. (It must be admitted that in his later works he did include the Renaissance.) Just as fervent admirers of classical architecture in the 17th century applied the nickname "Gothic" to the medieval buildings that seemed so barbarous to them (cf. p. 74), so our Victorian ancestors two centuries later labelled the "un-English" and fantastic churches and palaces erected between *c.* 1600 and *c.* 1750 (especially in the Roman Catholic countries of Southern and Central Europe) as "Baroque," because it was the most offensive nickname then available. Ruskin had already branded the Renaissance as a "foul torrent," and some more emphatic term of abuse was required to describe an even lower form of art.

Writing another century later, when this word Baroque has passed into our language as a specific and intelligible term, accepted without question by serious scholars, it would seem unnecessary to provide this explanation; but the Victorian prejudice against the style lingers on, in spite of several books on the subject that have appeared since 1912, when the first attempt to describe it in English was published.[1]

As remarked in the previous chapter, the Baroque movement in architecture was a revolt against the pedantry of the schoolmen—e.g. Vignola, Palladio, Scamozzi—who in their various books advocated a return to a more strict revival of classical Roman architecture and the "orders"; though Vignola's delightful Villa Giulia (p. 111) is far from being a mere reproduction of antique models. The beginnings of Baroque have been traced by some critics to Michelangelo, with his natural painter's and sculptor's taste for the picturesque, but it did not blossom into full flower until the early years of the 17th century and its effects were first felt in Rome. Pope Sixtus V (1585–90), with Domenico Fontana as his architect, had already begun the process of beautifying

[1] M. S. Briggs, *Baroque Architecture* (1912); also in German (1914).

and remodelling the city, which had now recovered from the Sack of Rome in 1527 and was displaying much of its former splendour. When I first visited Rome in 1907 it was a surprise to me to find how small a part the classical ruins played in the general landscape or "townscape," as seen, for instance, in the familiar panoramas from the Pincian or Janiculan hills; and indeed at that date the Baroque movement was hardly mentioned in the standard textbooks. During the ensuing half-century the prospect has changed again—thanks largely to Mussolini and his megalomania (see Chapter 13); but even so Rome within the walls remains essentially a Baroque city.

During the 17th century it was not, of course, the capital of Italy, because there was no country of Italy. Rome was merely the seat of the powerful Papacy and the capital of the Papal States, which extended from Terracina to Grosseto on the west coast, from Fermo nearly to Venice on the east coast—thus including Ferrara, Bologna, Ravenna and Viterbo, among towns mentioned in this book. South of the Papal States lay the "Kingdom of Naples," which was a Spanish possession until 1713 and then passed to the Hapsburg emperors of Austria until 1734, when it reverted to the Spanish Bourbons as the "Kingdom of the Two Sicilies."

North of the Papal States were the Grand Duchies of Tuscany (including Florence, Pisa and Siena), Savoy (including Turin), Milan, Parma, Modena, etc.; also the republics of Venice and Genoa. These political divisions naturally influenced the Baroque architecture of southern and northern Italy, which will be treated separately in the next two chapters.

Returning to Rome, the reader will notice from the long list on pp. 131-2 that the Baroque buildings there consisted mostly of churches large and small, of palaces and villas erected mainly by leading papal families, and of minor works of civic embellishment such as fountains. Of the architects concerned in these numerous and often vast projects the two names appearing most prominently in the list are those of Bernini and Borromini.

Giovanni Lorenzo Bernini (1598–1680) was born in Naples, the son of a Florentine sculptor then working there. When he was still only a boy he went to Rome in 1604 or 1605, and there carved two portrait busts of such surprising excellence that he soon earned the patronage of several powerful cardinals, and ultimately came to be employed by the Pope himself. Thereafter he took a leading part in the transformation of Rome. Once settled there Bernini naturally studied the sculpture of Michelangelo, with its tendency to realism and occasionally to exaggeration; also the lively and pagan work of Giovanni da Bologna, whose "Rape of the Sabines" (1583, now at Florence) may well have inspired Bernini's "Rape of Proserpine." This latter work was one of several executed between 1612 and 1622, the others including "David," "Aeneas and Anchises" and "Apollo and Daphne" (all these now in the Villa Borghese at Rome). His masterpiece was "The Ecstasy of St Teresa" (1646, in the church of S. Maria della Vittoria, Rome). This work in particular— with its incredibly realistic skill, its miraculous representation of warm human flesh in cold marble, its sense of life and movement and its cleverly contrived lighting—is the obvious ancestor of all those whirling, gesticulating and yet brilliantly executed statues which balance themselves on lofty parapets or perch on high altars in churches all over Bavaria, Austria and other Catholic countries as well as in Baroque Italy.

Besides these Bernini modelled or carved many fine portrait busts, among which that of Cardinal Scipio Borghese, his patron (1632, in the Villa Borghese), is typical.

In the tomb of Pope Alexander VII in St Peter's, Rome, Bernini introduced a novelty, a skeleton among a luscious bevy of nymphs—a crude reminder of mortality that set a fashion for many later memorials (and that in parti-coloured marbles, surely his worst effort).

Midway between sculpture and architecture are his beautiful fountains: of the Four Rivers and of the Triton in the Piazza Navona, of the Triton in the Piazza Bar-berini, one in the Piazza di S. Pietro, others in the Villa Mattei, the Palazzo Antamoro, the Vatican Gardens and the Barberini Gardens; also the less successful Acqua Acetosa outside Rome and the rather ridiculous "Obelisk of the Elephant" in the Piazza Minerva.

As an architect Bernini was an exponent of the so-called "Barocco corruption" (Ruskin) in several features of St Peter's. His colossal *baldacchino* under the dome recalls a story related by his biographer Baldinucci to the effect that Bernini, while still a youth, was walking through the newly completed cathedral with Annibale Caracci, the painter, who remarked that some day an architect would have to be found to design an isolated high altar beneath the centre of the vast dome. Bernini replied, "Perhaps I shall be that man!" and, as it happened in due course, in 1633 he was. His overpowering bronze *baldacchino*, 95 feet high, is cast in metal rifled from the roof of the Pan-theon (cf. p. 24); and its four enormous twisted and heavily decorated columns are said to be based on late Roman prototypes. This huge structure has occasioned much hostile criticism; but it is significant that something very like it is being provided in our own St Paul's in London as the best solution of an admittedly difficult problem.

At the side of St Peter's Bernini built the Scala Regia (Royal Staircase), the width of which diminishes from the entrance inwards, thus creating the illusion of increased length—a typical Baroque trick.

The superb quasi-elliptical colonnade surrounding the Piazza di S. Pietro (1656–66) has escaped hostile criticism even from those who detest the Baroque. It has been said that Bernini intended to destroy the quarter known as "the Borgo" and then to drive a wide avenue from the end of his colonnade past the Castle of S. Angelo to the Ponte S. Angelo over the Tiber. This project, never achieved in his lifetime, was ultimately accomplished under Mussolini in 1935, with results that have been severely condemned in many quarters (see pp. 160, 163).

According to one authority Bernini himself made models for 22 of the 62 colossal statues which surmount the colonnade. Apart from St Peter's he designed the handsome church of S. Andrea al Quirinale in Rome (1658–70); also other churches at Ariccia (1664) and Castel Gandolfo (1660) in the Alban Hills not far away—both these for the Pope.

Of his secular buildings in Rome the most important are the Palazzo di Montecitorio, near the Corso, and the Palazzo Barberini. He began building the former for the Ludovisi family in 1650; but it was completed for Innocent XII by Carlo Fontana, who modified the original design. Since 1870 it has housed the Chamber of Deputies, and has been somewhat altered.

The Palazzo Barberini is a joint work of Carlo Maderno (the designer of the feeble façade of St Peter's), who began it in 1624; of Borromini, who followed him; and finally of Bernini, so that the two rival protagonists of the Baroque in Rome here found themselves jointly responsible for a famous building. The wonderful spiral staircase is Borromini's work.

Bernini had become so famous by 1665 that Cardinal Mazarin wrote to him from France, offering him a post in the royal service with a salary of 12,000 crowns a year, But the Pope objected, saying that "Bernini was made for Rome, and Rome for Bernini." Then Louis XIV, Le Roi Soleil, himself wrote to Bernini in terms of flattering eulogy, congratulating him upon the designs he had just made for the new Louvre, and begging him to honour Paris with his presence. Eventually the great architect, now 68 years of age, set out on his journey. He was treated like royalty as he passed through Tuscany, Turin and Lyons, "so that he was accustomed to compare himself with an elephant, or some *lusus naturae*. The nunzio went out of Paris with relays of horses to receive him, and he was conducted to the royal palace like one about to dispense happiness to the nation."[1]

Yet all this splendid reception led to nothing, as the design for the new Louvre was never carried out; but news of his triumphal progress reached one Dr Christopher Wren (then beginning to abandon science for architecture), who managed to arrange an interview in Paris with the great man. "Bernini's design for the Louvre I would have given my skin for," Wren wrote to a friend in England, "but the old reserved Italian gave me but a few minutes' View. It was five little Designs on paper, for which he hath received as many pistoles. I had only

[1] F. Milizia, *Le Vite dei più celebri Architetti* (1768). Eng. trans. E. Cresy (1826). Vol. ii, p. 217.

Time to copy it in my Fancy and Memory, and shall be able by Discourse and a Crayon to give you a tolerable account of it."[1]

Bernini was no sycophant, and was a tremendous worker, who objected to any trivial interruption of whatever project he might have in hand; and on one such occasion when he had gone into a brown study before an incomplete study he said: "Do not touch me; I am in love." Looking at the marble nymphs he produced, one can believe it!

Bernini is represented in England by several works: the marble group of Neptune and Glaucus, about 6 feet high and with typical wind-blown drapery, at Brocklesby Park, Lincolnshire; a portrait bust of "Mr Baker (?)" in the Victoria and Albert Museum; a marble portrait bust of Charles I (1637) at Windsor Castle; and a number of drawings in the Windsor Castle collection.

His rival, Francesco Borromini (1599–1667), was his junior by a year, and was born at Bissone near Lugano. He arrived in Rome as a youth c. 1617, and worked there as an architect, first for Maderno and then for Bernini. Unlike Bernini and many other successful Italian architects he never practised painting or sculpture seriously, but started and continued as an architect pure and simple. If his success was a trifle less spectacular than Bernini's it was nevertheless striking enough. He too received a generous meed of praise during his lifetime. Pope Urban VIII (Maffeo Barberini) created him a Cavaliere di Cristo besides awarding him a pension and huge fees. The King of Spain gave him the Cross of St James, together with enormous fees for designing a royal palace which

[1] For more about this incident see M. S. Briggs, *Wren the Incomparable* (1953), p. 41.

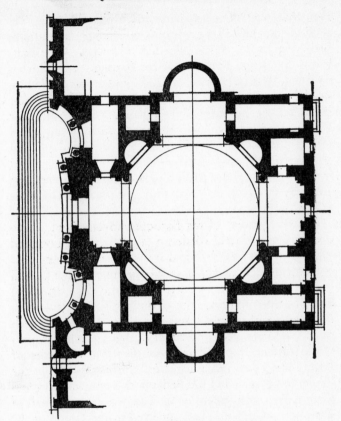

S. Agnese, Piazza Navona, Rome: Plan

was never built. Among 19th-century critics of architecture Borromini's name was always mentioned as the arch-villain of the "Barocco corruption"; and indeed he was more of a revolutionary than Bernini, delighting in curved lines, twisted columns, contorted figures and in fact every sort of eccentricity that broke the rules. Yet with all this he had a genius for producing successful as well as dramatic effects, whether of form or of colour. From the latest writers on the Baroque style he has received much appreciation and praise. His buildings, nearly all in Rome, are listed on pp. 131–2; to these must be added the beautiful Villa Falconieri at Frascati near Rome (1638–41), which served as a German headquarters during the Second World War, and therefore suffered considerable damage by bombing. As for his internal transformation of the basilica of S. Giovanni in Laterano at Rome (c. 1650), that must strain the loyalty of his most fervent admirers.

Of other leaders of the Baroque movement in Rome the chief were Carlo Maderno (1556–1629), a Lombard whose work at St Peter's and at the Palazzo Barberini has been mentioned; and at least two members of the Lunghi or Longhi family of architects—Onorio (c. 1569–1619) and his son Martino the Younger (1602–57), who between them designed and completed the fine church of S. Carlo al Corso and sundry other churches. Meanwhile further improvements in the civic amenities of Rome had taken place, e.g. the "Spanish Steps" in the Piazza di Spagna, and the Fontana di Trevi; the first and almost the only example of Rococo (as opposed to Baroque) architecture had appeared in the façade of the ancient basilica of S. Croce; and the last phase of the Baroque movement may be seen in the rather ponderous façades of S. Maria Maggiore and of S. Giovanni in Laterano. In 1750 or so the Roman stage is all set for a rather half-hearted return to classical rectitude.

PLATE XI

Venice: S. Maria della Salute, exterior (*Photo by courtesy of the Italian State Tourist Office*)

PLATE XII

Genoa: The University, cortile

BAROQUE, ETC., BUILDINGS IN ROME
(c. 1600–1750)

1597–1603	S. Susanna, façade and interior	C. Maderno
1603	Palazzo Rospigliosi	F. Ponzio
1605–53	S. Andrea delle Fratte (façade and campanile later)	?
1606–12	St Peter's, nave and façade	Maderno
1608–13	S. Sebastiano	Ponzio & Vasanzio
1610	Palazzo Sciarra-Colonna	Ponzio
1612	Acqua Paola	,,
1612–13	Casino Borghese	Vasanzio
1612–90	S. Carlo al Corso (dome later)	O. & M. Longhi
1613–15	Villa (now Galleria) Borghese	M. Longhi & Vasanzio
1614	S. Trinità dei Pellegrini	?
1615	Palazzo Mattei	Maderno
1624–33	St Peter's, *baldacchino*	Bernini
1625	S. Bibiana rebuilt	,,
1626	(St Peter's dedicated)	
1626–33	Palazzo Barberini	Bernini, Maderno & Borromini
1626–75	S. Ignazio (façade by Algardi later)	O. Grassi
1628–47	St Peter's, tomb of Urban VIII	Bernini
1629–33	S. Gregorio Magno	G. B. Soria
1635–50	SS. Martina e Luca	P. da Cortona
c. 1637	Triton fountain, Piazza Barberini	Bernini
1637–40	S. Filippo Neri	Borromini
1638–41	S. Carlo alle Quattro Fontane	,,
c. 1640	Palazzo Falconieri	,,
1642	Palazzo Madama	Marucelli
1642–50	S. Ivo alla Sapienza	Borromini
1644–50	Villa Doria-Pamfili	A. Algardi
1646–50	SS. Vincenzo ed Anastasio	M. Longhi II
1648–51	Fountain of Four Rivers, Piazza Navona	Bernini

1650	Palazzo Pamfili (now Doria-Pamfili)	
		Rainaldi & Borromini
c. 1650	S. Maria delle Sette Dolori	Borromini
1650 on	Palazzo Montecitorio	Bernini
1652 on	S. Agnese, Piazza Navona	
		Rainaldi & Borromini
1655	Porta del Popolo, inner side	Bernini
1656–7	S. Maria della Pace	P. da Cortona
1656–66	St Peter's, chair of St Peter	Bernini
„	„ peristyle and colonnade	„
1658–62	S. Maria in Via Lata	P. da Cortona
1658–70	S. Andrea al Quirinale	Bernini
1661	Acqua Acetosa	„
1662–4	Collegio del Propaganda Fide	Borromini
1662–79	S. Maria di Monte Santo	Rainaldi & Bernini
„	S. Maria de' Miracoli	„
1663	Vatican Palace: Scala Regia	Bernini
1663–7	S. Maria in Campitelli	Rainaldi
c. 1665	Palazzo Aste-Bonaparte	G. A. de' Rossi
1667	"Elephant Obelisk," Piazza Minerva	Bernini
1668 on	S. Carlo al Corso, dome	P. da Cortona
1670	Palazzo Altieri	G. A. de' Rossi
1673	S. Maria Maggiore, rear façade	Rainaldi
1700	Palazzo Bolognetti	C. Fontana
1702–24	SS. Apostoli	„
1723–5	Scala di Spagna ("Spanish Steps")	F. de' Sanctis
1733–6	S. Giovanni in Laterano, main façade	A. Galilei
1734	S. Giovanni dei Fiorentini	„ „
1735	Fontana di Trevi	N. Salvi
1736	Palazzo della Consulta	F. Fuga
1737–60 ?	Villa Albani (now Torlonia)	C. Marchionni
1741–3	S. Maria Maggiore, main façade	F. Fuga
1743–4	S. Croce in Gerusalemme, rebuilt in	
	Rococo style	D. Gregorini & P. Passalacqua
1749	S. Maria degli Angeli, remodelled	L. Vanvitelli
1750	S. Apollinare rebuilt	Fuga

10

Baroque Architecture
in Northern Italy

c. 1600 – c. 1750

AS EXPLAINED IN the previous chapter (p. 123), Italy
north of Rome was divided throughout the Baroque
period into a number of autonomous units: the Papal
States, the republics of Genoa and Venice and several
Grand Duchies. The impact of the Baroque movement
was felt in varying degree in these different territories and
most strongly in the city of Turin, capital of the Duchy of
Savoy which was merged in the Kingdom of Sardinia
after 1718, with its duke as King of Sardinia.

In the city of Genoa the tradition of fine palace design
set by Alessi in the 16th century (p. 114) was developed on magnificent lines by the architect Baccio di
Bartolomeo Bianco (c. 1580–c. 1651), a native of Como,
who began his career as a painter. Later he turned to
architecture and attracted the notice of the powerful
Genoese family of Balbi, who became his patrons from
1609 onwards. For them he designed three noble palaces
in the Via Balbi, viz. the Università (originally started as

133

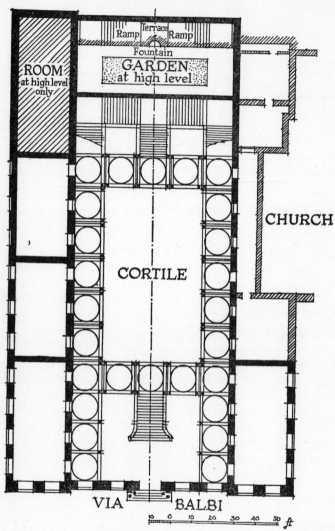

ROOM
at high level
only

Ramp Terrace Ramp

Fountain

GARDEN
at high level

CHURCH

CORTILE

VIA   BALBI

10 0 10 20 30 40 50 ft

Genoa: The Università: Plan

a Jesuit college and built in 1623 onwards at the cost of
the Jesuit Paolo Balbi); the Palazzo Balbi-Durazzo-
Pallavicini (1620); and the Palazzo Balbi-Senarega (begun
in 1609). These three mansions, of which the first-named
was seriously damaged by bombing in the Second World
War, were all superbly planned, with splendid staircases
which served as models for several London clubs built by
Sir Charles Barry and other famous English architects
two centuries later. Bianco had also been appointed
municipal architect for Genoa in 1620, and in that capacity
may have designed the Porta Pila (1633). His other work
includes the handsome Villa Durazzo (1620) east of the
city.

Other large buildings of this period in Genoa were the
Palazzo Reale (Royal Palace) in the Via Balbi (1650–7)
by two Lombard architects, G. A. Falcone and P. F. Can-
tone, and the enormous Albergo dei Poveri (= hostel for
the poor), commanding the whole city like a fortress,
built by four different architects between 1655 and 1675;
but neither of these buildings compares in architectural
interest or importance with the work of Bianco.

The city of Venice contains several notable Baroque
churches and palaces, listed on pp. 141–2. These aroused
the bitterest hostility from Ruskin, who described the
Baroque phase as the "Grotesque Renaissance" in architecture, and wrote thus of a carved head on one of the
churches: "In that head is embodied the type of the evil
spirit to which Venice was abandoned in the fourth
period of her decline, and it is well that we should see and
feel the full horror of it on this spot, and know what
pestilence it was that came and breathed upon her beauty
until it melted away."

Yet the Baroque seems to harmonize very happily with

K

the general atmosphere of historical Venice; and certainly the beautiful church of S. Maria della Salute—her finest Baroque building—has become an essential feature in her marvellous architectural scenery. In the 17th and 18th centuries Venice had lost much of her overseas territory east of the Adriatic to Turkey, and much of her former

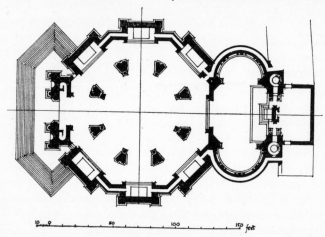

S. Maria della Salute, Venice: Plan

trade to her rival Genoa; but she had become what she has remained ever since—a city of pleasure as well as of maritime trade; and the accumulated riches of her patrician merchants were available for every form of gaiety and display. Tourists from all over Europe flocked into the city as a show-place, and were welcomed with endless pageants, masques, balls, "serenades," performances at the opera—but not, as nowadays, with miles of bathing-huts along the Lido. Young Englishmen of noble birth making the "Grand Tour" were received by the Doge himself and personally conducted round St Mark's. Picnics were organized alfresco to the gay villas lining the banks of the Brenta Canal between Venice (Mestre) and Padua (p. 138).

The influence of Palladio still pervaded Venice at the beginning of the 17th century, and may be traced in the work of her most distinguished Baroque architect, Baldassare Longhena (1598–1682), who was born in the city and died there. Unlike most of the Italian architects mentioned hitherto in this book he began as a mason, and was then trained in architecture by the scholarly (or pedantic) Scamozzi; but there is nothing pedantic in his masterpiece, the magnificent church of S. Maria della Salute (1631–82), one of the greatest buildings in Italy and indeed in all Europe. Even Ruskin had to admit, grudgingly, that it possessed some merits.[1] Longhena seems to have realized the unique importance of the site, at the mouth of the Grand Canal facing St Mark's, and he utilized his opportunity with real genius.

His two great palaces on the Grand Canal—the Palazzo Rezzonico (1650), to which a storey was added after his death, and the Palazzo Pesaro (1679–1710)—carry on the tradition of Palladio, Sansovino and Sanmicheli with an added grandeur; and, for all their classical sobriety, blend with the older palaces lining the canal. Longhena's work also included the monastic buildings of S. Giorgio Maggiore.

The other leading architect of the Baroque period, Giuseppe Sardi or Salvi (1630–99), born near Lugano, added an exuberant façade to Longhena's church of S. Maria ai Scalzi (1649 onwards) near the station; and also

---

[1] I selected this building as frontispiece for my book, *Baroque Architecture*, in 1912; and would do the same again today.

to the churches of S. Salvatore and of S. Maria del Giglio, otherwise known as S. Maria Zobenigo. His work lacks all the dignity of Longhena's. Apart from churches and palaces another small building merits mention as part of the Venetian scene—the Dogana or Custom House (1676–82) near the Salute; but it is not particularly Baroque in character. The Palazzo Labia (1720–50), by A. Cominelli, contains magnificent Baroque architectural frescoes by G. B. Tiepolo.

In the gay society of the 17th–18th centuries the wealthier citizens of Venice repaired annually to their country villas on the mainland. These lined the banks of the Brenta Canal leading from Mestre to Padua, the fashion having been set by Palladio with his Villa Malcontenta (c. 1560). Most of them are, indeed, very simple in design externally, and many of them rather shabby; but the great Villa Pisani at Strà (1735), now a national monument, retains much of its former glory and is well worth a visit. The annual exodus of the Venetian nobility and plutocracy to these country mansions was called *villeggiatura*. The country between Venice, Treviso, Udine and Vicenza is dotted with handsome villas of the 18th century, all in the tradition of Palladio and Scamozzi.

Without going to Venice one can obtain some idea of its splendour and colour in the late Baroque period from the paintings of Canaletto (1697–1768) and Guardi (1712–93), many of which are in London galleries.

Notable Baroque buildings in Milan are not very numerous (see list, pp. 142–3); and the best of them were all designed by Francesco Maria Ricchini or Ricchino (d. 1652), of whose life singularly little is known. His churches include S. Giuseppe, S. Antonio Abbate, S. Giovanni alle Case Rotte, the upper part of S. Maria alla

Porta and the restoration of S. Giorgio. The last-named is a charming little octagonal church of Baroque type with an attractive façade; but the others are of no architectural importance, and Ricchini's reputation rests entirely upon his palaces, though he did complete Tibaldi's work on the west front of Milan Cathedral in 1605–38.

The Ospedale Maggiore had been begun by the Florentine Antonio Filarete in 1457; and when it fell to Ricchini to design its magnificent central *cortile* (280 feet by 220 feet) in 1621 he was evidently influenced by the Early Renaissance character of its style.

The Palazzo Brera, now a famous picture-gallery, was erected originally in 1651–86 as a Jesuit college from Ricchini's designs. It is a noble building with a bold and dignified façade and a splendid *cortile*, surrounded by two tiers of arcading—Doric above and Ionic below, the columns being coupled. There is nothing "grotesque" in his architecture, which maintains the scholarly austerity of the "Mannerist" school described in Chapter VIII. His buildings in Milan include the Palazzi Annoni (1631), Litta (formerly Arese, 1648, but façade later) and Duroni; also, probably, the Collegio Elvetico (1627, with a curved façade), which became the Archivio; and the picturesque gateway of the Seminario Arcivescovile.

In Turin the Baroque arrived late but had a spectacular harvest. It is still the capital of Piedmont, but in the 17th–18th centuries formed part of the independent Duchy of Savoy, which produced the first monarch when Italy became a united kingdom in 1860. The Duchy of Savoy comprised several districts which had been French before the 17th century; and there is a marked French influence in the character of the Baroque architecture of Turin. Its products (listed pp. 142–3) were mostly the work of two extremely gifted architects, Guarini and Juvara. Camillo-Guarino Guarini (*b*. Modena, 1624; *d*. Milan, 1688) was originally a Theatine monk who also functioned as a professor of mathematics, philosophy and literature while practising architecture and, presumably, sundry religious duties. Besides his buildings in Turin he also designed the eccentric church of S. Gregorio at Messina in Sicily (destroyed by earthquake in 1908) and the Theatine church of St Anne at Paris (1662, since destroyed). Together with Francesco Borromini, already mentioned (pp. 128–30), and the Jesuit priest and architectural draughtsman Andrea Pozzo (1642–1709) he formed one of the trio of Baroque architects whose work has aroused the fiercest unfavourable criticism. It may or may not be significant that two of this trio were clerical amateurs.

Of Guarini's numerous buildings in Turin the huge Palazzo Carignano (1680) is the most important, and exhibits most of the defects and some of the merits of the Baroque style. Curved lines abound in its design, and its central feature is an oval block containing a magnificent staircase. In this palace was born Vittorio Emanuele II (1820–78), the first king of United Italy, whose name appears all over the country on monuments of varying merit and in countless streets and squares.

Filippo Juvara or Juvarra (1676–1736) was likewise a priest before he turned to architecture. He then studied under Carlo Fontana in Rome. Besides his numerous important buildings listed on p. 143 he designed the domes of Como Cathedral and of S. Andrea at Mantua. Outside Italy he made designs for the royal palace at Madrid in Spain (carried out by his pupil Sacchetti in 1738–64); for royal palaces at Lisbon and Mafra in Portugal; and for Lisbon Cathedral.

Outside Milan, Genoa and Venice there are relatively few important buildings of the 17th–18th centuries north of Rome; but the list on p. 142 mentions examples in Bologna and the Marches.

BAROQUE BUILDINGS IN GENOA
AND DISTRICT
(c. 1600–c. 1750)

1609 on	Palazzo Balbi-Senarega	B. Bianco
1620	Palazzo Durazzo-Pallavicini	,,
,,	Villa Durazzo, near Genoa	,,
1623 on	Palazzo dell' Università	,,
1633	Porta Pila	B. Bianco (?)
1650–7	Palazzo Reale, Via Balbi	Falcone & Cantone
1655–75	Albergo dei Poveri	Several architects
1731	S. Torpete	A. Ricca

BAROQUE, ETC., BUILDINGS IN VENICE
AND VENETIA
(c. 1600–c. 1750)

1609	Verona. Gran Guardia Vecchia	Curtoni
1631–82	Venice. S. Maria della Salute	B. Longhena
1643–5	,, Monastery of S. Giorgio Maggiore	,,
1649	,, Church of Gli Scalzi	Sardi & Longhena
1650	,, Palazzo Rezzonico (top storey 1745)	Longhena
1663	,, S. Salvatore, façade added to	Sardi
1668	,, S. Moisè	A. Tremignan
1673	,, S. Lazzaro, façade of	Sardi
1676–82	,, Dogana di Mare	Benoni
1678–1709	,, S. Eustachio (façade later)	Grassi
1679–1710	,, Palazzo Pesaro	Longhena
1680	,, S.M. del Giglio (S.M. Zobenigo)	Sardi
1688	,, Palazzo Fini (now Grand Hotel)	?

1718–38	Venice. SS. Simeone e Giuda	Scalfaretti
1720–50	,, Palazzo Labia	A. Cominelli
1725–36	,, Church of the Gesuati	G. Massari
1735	Strà. Villa Pisani F. M. Preti & G. Frigimelica	

BAROQUE BUILDINGS IN BOLOGNA, THE MARCHES, ETC.
(c. 1600–c. 1750)

1611–36	Bologna. S. Paolo G. A. Magenta & E. Fichi
1627–73	Parma. Palazzo Municipale G. B. Magnani
1634	Modena. Palazzo Ducale (damaged in Second World War) Avanzini
1637–1728	Ferrara. Duomo (in part) L. Danesi & F. Mazzarelli
1687–1787	Bologna. S. Maria della Vita (dome 1787 by Bibiena) G. B. Bergonzoni
1723	,, Santuario della Madonna di S. Luca C. F. Dotti
1750–4	Loreto. Campanile at the Casa Santa Vanvitelli

BAROQUE BUILDINGS IN LOMBARDY AND PIEDMONT
(c. 1600–c. 1750)

1602	Milan. S. Alessandro (façade later) L. Binago
1607–30	,, S. Giuseppe Ricchino
1609 on	Turin. Church of Corpus Domini, altered 1753 Guarini
1620–1	Milan. Ospedale Maggiore, Great Court Ricchino
1627	,, Collegio Elvetico (Archivio dello Stato) ,,
?	,, Seminario, entrance gateway ,,
1633–50	Turin. Castello Valentino A. di Castellamonte
1646	,, Palazzo Reale begun ,,

1648	Milan. Palazzo del Brera	Ricchino
1663–9	Turin. Town hall	Lanfranco (Lanfranchi)
1667–90	„ Cathedral, chapel of S. Sindone	Guarini
1668–87	„ S. Lorenzo	„
1679	„ Palazzo dell' Accademie	„
„	„ S. Croce	Lanfranco
1679 on	„ S. Filippo (façade 1891)	
		Guarini, then Juvara
1680	„ Palazzo Carignano	Guarini
Early 18th c.	„ Santuario della Consolata	
		Guarini, then Juvara
1712 on	Rivoli near Turin. Castello	Juvara
1713	Turin. University	A. Ricca
1717–31	„ La Superga	Juvara
1718–21	„ Palazzo Madama, additions	„
1718–72	„ S. Cristina: façade	„
1729	„ Palazzo Cavour	J. J. Plantieri
?	„ Palazzo Saluzzo-Paesana	„
1729–33	Stupinigi near Turin. Castello	Juvara
1731	Como Cathedral, dome	„
1733	Mondovi. Santuario	F. Gallo
1737	Collegno near Turin. Certosa	Juvara
?	Turin. Palazzo Ferrero d'Ormea	Juvara (?)
1746	Brescia. S. Maria della Pace	G. Massari

II

Baroque Architecture
in Southern Italy and Sicily

c. 1600 - *c.* 1750

BEFORE THE UNIFICATION of Italy as a kingdom in
1860–1, southern Italy (including Sicily) had formed the
"Kingdom of Naples"—under Spanish Bourbon kings
and their viceroys—from 1503 to 1707; then it became a
part of the Austrian dominions till 1734, when it reverted
to Spanish rule. Thus Spanish influence appears in its
architecture, and Baroque architecture was very popular
in Spain. Although there are many Baroque buildings in
Naples, Palermo, Syracuse and Catania—the chief cities
of southern Italy and Sicily—which are listed on pp.
147–50, the most important contribution that southern
Italy and Sicily make to my story consists in their
possession of four towns where Baroque architecture pre-
dominates over everything else; Lecce, in the "heel" of
Italy and in the province of Apulia; Noto, Modica and
Ragusa in the south-east corner of Sicily. It is not clear to
me why Lecce, which is a very ancient town but not a
seaport and is in a very remote corner of Italy, should

have produced so remarkable a crop of buildings in the 17th century; but the present town of Noto was built entirely afresh in 1703 onwards, after an earthquake in 1683 had destroyed an earlier town of the same name which stood 5 miles away on an ancient Greek site; and much the same events occurred on the same occasion at Ragusa and Modica. As for Messina, it too was very rich in Baroque architecture until the greater part of the city was destroyed by an earthquake in 1908.

Lecce was practically unknown in England fifty years ago, though the German scholar Gregorovius (1821–91) had described it as "the Florence of Apulia"; but in 1907 the then editor of the *Architectural Review* commissioned me to visit the city and write some articles for him about it. These were followed by my book, *In the Heel of Italy*, published in 1910, and afterwards, in 1912, in an Italian translation under the title *Nel Tallone d'Italia.*

Lecce is a gay, clean, bright city, with a present population of about 66,000, standing in a rather arid plain about 7 miles from the Adriatic coast. Planes flying from Athens to London via Munich pass right over it. It remains unscathed by the Second World War. All its historical buildings are of a local limestone which has kept its golden colour through the centuries, and there is a pleasant public garden. The architects chiefly responsible for its numerous Baroque buildings were Giuseppe Zimbalo (1659–95), commonly called "Zingarello" (= little gipsy), Francesco Zimbalo, and their pupil Giuseppe Cino, who also practised sculpture. The various 17th–18th-century churches in Lecce vary in style from the ornate and fantastic (e.g. S. Croce and the Carmine) to the comparatively sedate (e.g. S. Irene). The smaller palaces are of great originality, delicacy and charm.

Paul Bourget in his *Sensations d'Italie* (1891) sums up Lecce very neatly (my translation): "It is so seductive, such a precious jewel of a town. . . . Before coming here, I attached to the terms 'baroque' and 'rococo' no other meaning than that of unpleasing pretentiousness. Lecce has shown me that they can also be synonymous with gay fancy, with playful elegance and with merry grace. . . . Here one dreams of light music, of masquerades, of voluptuous feasts, of a happy and Italianized Spain." These comments could also be applied in some measure to both Noto and Ragusa; but the case of the larger cities is somewhat different.

The cathedral at Syracuse (Siracusa) has as its core a Greek Doric temple of the 5th century B.C., which was converted into a church in A.D. 640, then into a mosque in 878, then again into a church, and was finally re-modelled in Baroque style after the great earthquake of 1693 already mentioned. It is therefore a heterogeneous mixture, externally and internally. The cathedral at Messina, originally built in the late 11th century by the Norman rulers of Sicily (p. 58), was "modernized" in 1682, but an earthquake destroyed most of the building, and the earthquake of 1908 completed its destruction.

The Baroque buildings of Palermo (listed on p. 149) are chiefly notable for the remarkable figure sculpture in stucco by Giacomo Serpotta found in several churches, e.g. S. Zita, S. Lorenzo and S. Matteo.

On the Italian mainland the famous Baroque church at Montecassino, erected in 1637–1727 to replace the ancient building founded by St Benedict, was utterly destroyed in the Second World War. It was designed by Cosimo Fansago or Fanzaga (1591–1678), a Lombard architect whose work is also to be seen in two churches

PLATE XIII

Lecce: S. Croce, façade (*Photo: Alinari*)

PLATE XIV

Rome: Monument to Vittorio Emanuele (*Photo: Alinari*)

Rome: University

at Naples, S. Martino and S. Maria Maggiore. Of the
other Baroque buildings of Naples mentioned on p. 148,
though some are very large none is of any great architectural importance. The church of SS. Annunziata (1757–
1782) is the work of Luigi Vanvitelli (1700–73), a native
of the city, whose immense and immensely important
royal palace at Caserta (1751–64), with its dramatic
"Cascade," is one of the outstanding examples of late
Baroque architecture in Italy.

BAROQUE BUILDINGS IN SOUTHERN
ITALY, excluding Sicily
(c. 1600 – c. 1750)

Caserta	1751–64	Royal Palace and Cascade	Vanvitelli
Lecce	1549–1695	S. Croce	G. Zimbalo, etc.
„	1591–1639	S. Irene (Benedictine) M. Coluzio	
„	1606	S. Maria delle Grazie	„
„	1630	Church of the Scalzi	„
„	1646 on	Prefettura (formerly convent)	Zimbalo
„	1659–82	Duomo, remodelling and campanile	„
„	1663	S. Angelo (façade unfinished),	„
„	1681–3	Column of S. Oronzo	„
„	1687	S. Chiara	—
„	1691–1728	Church of the Rosario	Zimbalo
„	1694–1709	Seminario	G. Cino
„	1700	S. Matteo rebuilt	M. Carducci
„	1703	Porta Rusce rebuilt	—
„	1706–11	Church of the Carmine rebuilt	G. Cino
„	1708	Church of the Alcantarine	„
„	1710	SS. Nicolò e Cataldo, façade	„

Montecassino	1637–1727	Church of Benedictine Abbey (completely destroyed in Second World War) C. Fanzago
Naples	1600–41	Palazzo Reale (extended) 1752 D. Fontana
,,	1605	Jesuit College (afterwards university) G. da Nola
,,	c. 1630	S. Martino, church and cloister C. Fanzago
,,	1657	S. Maria Maggiore ,,
,,	1728	Palazzo Sanfelice F. Sanfelice
,,	1737	Teatro S. Carlo (façade 1839) Medrano & Carasale
,,	1738	Palazzo di Capodimonte Medrano
,,	1751	Reclusorio (Albergo dei Poveri) F. Fuga
,,	1757–82	SS. Annunziata Vanvitelli

BAROQUE BUILDINGS IN SICILY
(c. 1600 – c. 1750)

Catania	1730 on	Cathedral façade (in style of Juvara) Vaccarini
,,	1693–1735	S. Nicolò, church and convent Battaglio & Amato
,,	1732	Palazzo Municipale Vaccarini
,,	1735 on	S. Agata ,,
,,	1754	Collegio Cutelli ,,
Messina	c. 1662	S. Gregorio, façade (destroyed 1908) Guarini
,,	1682	Cathedral, remodelled (,,) —
Noto	1720–70	Cathedral (rebuilt after earthquake of 1693) —
,,	1727	S. Domenico R. Gagliardi (?)
,,	?	Church of the Carmine Gagliardi

Noto	?	S. Chiara	Gagliardi
,,	1737 on	Palazzo Astuto	—
,,	?	,, Frigintini	—
,,	?	,, Modica	—
,,	?	,, S. Giacomo	—
,,	?	,, Villadorata	P. Labisi
,,	1745 on	Church of the Immacolata	—
,,	1746	Palazzo Ducezio (later Municipio)	
			V. Sinatra
,,	,,	Palazzo Landolinda	—
,,	1750	Church of the Crocefissa	P. Labisi
Palermo	1586–1603	S. Zita	—
,,	1609–11	Quattro Canti	G. Lasso
,,	1612	S. Giuseppe dei Teatini (destroyed in Second World War)	—
,,	1626	Church of the Carmine Maggiore	
			V. la Barbara & M. Smiriglio
,,	1628	S. Salvatore (Norman church re-modelled)	G. Amato
,,	1632	S. Matteo	—
,,	1640	S. Domenico (façade 1726)	
			A. Cirincioni & T. Napoli
,,	?	La Martorana, Baroque façade	—
,,	1683	Gesù (former Jesuit church), seriously damaged in Second World War	—
,,	1686	Chiesa della Pietà	G. Amato
,,	1700	S. Agostino (older church re-modelled)	—
,,	1761	Piazza del Duomo, layout and statues	—
,,	1771	Palazzo Bonagia (damaged in Second World War)	—
,,	,,	Villa Giulia or "La Flora"	N. Palma
,,	1781 on	Duomo, new dome	F. Fuga
Ragusa	1590	S. Giuseppe, Baroque façade	—

Ragusa	1700	Palazzo Lupis	—
"	1706–60	Cathedral of S. Giovanni	—
"	18th c.	Casa Canonica adjoining cathedral	—
"	"	S. Maria dell' Idria	—
"	"	Palazzo Bertini	—
"	"	Palazzo Cosentini	—
"	1738–75	Basilica of S. Giorgio (dome 1820)	R. Gagliardi
Syracuse	1618	Palazzo Arcivescovile (altered 1751)	A. Vermexio (?)
"	?	S. Benedetto, façade	A. Vermexio (?)
"	c. 1628	Municipio	G. Vermexio
"	1635–87	Chiesa del Collegio	
"	1652–8	S. Maria	M. Bonamici
"	1693	S. Lucia alla Badia, façade	P. Picherali
"	1727	Church of Spirito Santo	"
"	1730–54	Duomo, new Baroque façade	A. Palma
"	18th c.	Palazzo Borgia, later Impellizzeri—	
"	"	Palazzo Beneventano del Bosco, façade	L. Ali

12

From Rococo to Fascismo

c. 1750 – *c.* 1922

THE LONG PERIOD of time covered by this chapter,
ending with the advent to power of Mussolini and his
fascist regime in 1922, was disturbed by several wars and
periods of civil unrest. At its beginning Italy as a country
did not exist. There was the Bourbon Kingdom of the
Two Sicilies in the south, the Papal States in the centre
and a number of autonomous republics in the north (cf.
p. 3). During 1796–1800 Napoleon's campaigns brought
war into Italy; there were insurrections and civil dis-
orders in 1820, 1848–50 and 1859; the wars of inde-
pendence in 1860–70 resulting in the unification of Italy;
the Abyssinian War, including the disastrous defeat at
Adowa in 1895–6; the war in Tripoli in 1911–12; indus-
trial strikes and rioting in 1914; the First World War in
1915–18; and finally Mussolini's introduction of fascism
and virtual dictatorship in 1922. Railways and their
stations were first built in the mid 19th century; and the
northern provinces of Italy were becoming industrialized
before that century ended. All these various factors had
some influence on the development of Italian architecture,

which in several respects did not follow contemporary trends in Western Europe and North America.

In those regions the last phase of Renaissance architecture proper gave way to a more academic and classical style of design, either Roman or Greek. Typical examples are the work of Nash (Regent Street, etc.), Burton (Athenaeum Club, London), Wilkins (University College and the National Gallery, London), Smirke (British Museum), Soane (Bank of England, London)—all in England; Playfair in Scotland; L. von Klenze in Berlin and Schinkel at Munich; Cameron in Russia; Bulfinch, Hoban, Latrobe and Thornton in the United States.

About 1840 or so this movement gave place to the "Gothic Revival" in most countries of Western and Central Europe, also in North America and in Australia. The course of events in Italy was different, and the Gothic Revival hardly made itself felt. As one looks across the vast prospect of roofs and domes from the terrace on the Pincio at Rome today, there is only one Gothic spire to be seen—that of G. E. Street's English church of All Saints (1887) just below; and a similar state of affairs exists in most other Italian cities.

As remarked on p. 130, there is an almost complete lack of Rococo buildings in Italy following the earlier Baroque of 1750 or so, and the later Baroque examples show a return to more austere classical models. The list of buildings on pp. 154–6 includes several built between 1805 and 1835 which are even more frankly academic, e.g. the Arco della Pace at Milan; the façade of the Teatro S. Carlo at Naples; the churches of Gran Madre di Dio at Turin and of S. Francesco di Paola at Naples (both copied more or less from the Pantheon at Rome); and the façade of S. Andrea delle Fratte at Rome. All these

are "antique" Roman rather than Greek. The Caffè
Pedrocchi at Padua (1831) is sometimes cited as a rare
example of "Greek Revival" design in Italy; but that
movement may also be detected in various features of
the Borghese Gardens in Rome, laid out in 1835 by
L. Canina and others.

The façade of the Central Railway Station in Milan, as
designed in 1857 by Bouchot, is a perfect specimen of the
French "Beaux Arts" style—not in the least Italian. Of all
the buildings of this long period of over 150 years, two
of the most aggressively hideous are in Piedmont; the
Mole Antonelliana, rising above the Synagogue at Turin;
and the domed spire of S. Gaudenzio at Novara. Both are
the work of Alessandro Antonelli (1798–1888). Even
allowing for the fickleness and impermanence of architectural fashions, it is difficult to concede any merits in
either design; but it is impossible to ignore them, for the
Mole Antonelliana is 538 feet high and the spire of S.
Gaudenzio 396 feet. A new type of architecture developed
during the 19th century in Italy as elsewhere is the
galleria or arcade of shops with a glass roof above:
examples are the Galleria Vittorio Emanuele at Milan
and the Galleria Umberto I at Naples (1887–90, by di
Mauro). Comment on these is needless.

Of other buildings listed on pp. 154–6 several are
merely dull, among them various blocks of government
offices; but special mention must be made of two su-
premely hideous examples: the Palazzo di Giustizia and
the Tempio Israelitico (or Synagogue), both in Rome.
Yet though these are inescapable objects in the prospect
of Rome from the Pincian terrace, there is one other
which cannot be forgotten or forgiven in any account of
the city's architecture, because it is the most prominent

and most strident of all—the immense monument to King Vittorio Emanuele II, on the north side of the Capitoline Hill and on the axis of the Corso and Via Flaminia. It is the outcome of an architectural competition held in 1884 and won by Giuseppe Sacconi (1854–1905) against 293 rivals. Although it was built in 1885–1911, and therefore antedates the era of megalomania inaugurated by Mussolini (see Chapter 13), it is obviously intended to proclaim from this ancient and magnificent site "the grandeur that was Rome"; and indeed it recaptures all the grandiloquence of the last days of the Empire. Its height is over 200 feet and, as it is entirely built of dazzling white marble, it dominates the whole city.

Less attractive in design and colour, but equally bombastic, is the Palazzo delle Belle Arti in the Valle Giulia (adjoining the British School at Rome, excellently designed by Sir Edwin Lutyens in 1911).

DATES OF VARIOUS BUILDINGS
(c. 1760 – 1922)

1777	Milan. Palazzo Belgiojoso	G. Piermarini
1777–8	„ La Scala Theatre	„
1777–80	Monza. Villa Reale	„
1790	Milan. Villa Reale, extensions	L. Pollak
1805	Rome. S. Pantaleo, façade	G. Valadier
1807	Milan. Arco della Pace, o del Sempione	
		L. Cagnola
„	Naples. Villa Floridiana	A. Niccolini
1809	Rome. Steps from Piazza del Popolo to Pincio	G. Valadier
1815	„ S. Rocco, façade (after Palladio)	„
„	Archway on Ponte Milvio	„
1816	Naples. Teatro S. Carlo, new façade	A. Niccolini

1817–32	Naples. S. Francesco di Paola (copy of Pantheon)	P. Banchi
1818–40	Turin. Church of Gran Madre di Dio (copy of Pantheon)	F. Bonsignore
1823–54	Rome. S. Paolo fuori, rebuilt after fire	L. Poletti & others
1826	„ S. Andrea delle Fratte, new façade	G. Valadier
1830–5	„ Villa Borghese gardens laid out	L. Canina
1831	Padua. Caffé Pedrocchi (in Greek styke)	G. Japelli
1850	Pavia. Great Hall of the university	G. Marchesi
1857–64	Milan. Central Railway Station (since rebuilt)	Bouchot
1863 on	Turin. Mole Antonelliana	A. Antonelli
1867–77	Milan. Galleria Vittorio Emanuele	G. Mengoni
1875–8	Turin. S. Gaudenzio, domed spire	A. Antonelli
1883	Rome, master plan for	A. Viviani
1884	„ Ministero delle Finanze	R. Canevari
„	„ Ministero della Guerra (War Office)	—
1885–1911	„ Monument to Vittorio Emanuele	G. Sacconi
1886–92	„ Banca d'Italia, Via Nazionale	G. Koch
1887	„ All Saints' (English) Church	G. E. Street
„	„ Church of the Sacro Cuore	V. Vespignani
1889–1910	„ Palazzo di Giustizia	G. Calderini
1890	„ Palazzo Margherita (ex Ludovisi)	G. Koch
1893	„ Policlinico (=general hospital)	G. Podesti
c. 1900	„ Palaces in Esedra di Termini	G. Koch
1902–5	„ Traforo (=tunnel) under Quirinale	A. Viviani
1904	„ Tempio Israelitico (=Synagogue)	Armanni & Costa

1908	Naples. Regia Università, façade	P. P. Quaglia
1911	Rome. Palazzo delle Belle Arti	C. Bazzani
,,	,, British School at Rome	Sir E. L. Lutyens
,,	,, Ponte Vittorio Emanuele	—
,,	,, Ponte del Risorgimento	—
1915–27	Milan. Città degli Studi (later university)	—

13

Architecture under Mussolini

1922-43

Benito Amilcare Andrea Mussolini, who became "Duce" (= "commander" or "leader"), the famous Italian dictator from 1922 to 1943, was born of humble parentage in an obscure village, and was successively school-teacher, agitator, editor, conscript and M.P. A book by an American journalist published in 1936 dealt with his sensational career under the title *Sawdust Caesar*, and in some respects that epithet was justified. A thick-set, bald-headed man, his proletarian figure was a gift to caricaturists, who pictured him as a bibulous and corpulent Caesar clad in a toga and crowned with a laurel wreath set slightly askew. That is one point of view; but when in Italy in 1926 and again in 1935 I heard him praised highly by two intelligent men who knew him well: one a cultured Englishman occupying a high position in Florence, the other an Italian senator of liberal sympathies and of academic distinction. His vulgarity and bombast and aggressiveness could have made no appeal whatever to either of them, yet both were favourably impressed by the many improvements he had made in Italy; among them the considerable influence that he had exerted in the replanning of Rome, in draining the malaria-ridden plain of the surrounding Campagna, in establishing modern garden cities in that desolate region, in clearing the ancient monuments of Rome from the shacks and vegetation that had grown over them like a fungus, in ridding the crowded streets of the noisy trams. I heard of him first as the man who had tidied up the cities and made the trains run to time; and indeed Italy was in a state of depression and exhaustion after the First World War had ended; it really did need a strong man to give the people encouragement and a bold lead.

So in 1922 he led the "March on Rome"—from the tail of the procession and in a comfortable sleeping-car of the Naples express—to save his country. Twenty-three years later, when the Second World War was in its last phase, he and his mistress Clara Petacci were kicked to death by an infuriated group of "partisans" as they were trying to escape from Italy into Switzerland. Unlike his rival, ally and protégé, Adolf Hitler, who had been frustrated in his attempts to become an architect, Mussolini had cherished no such early ambitions; but the tremendous influence that later he came to exert on Italian architecture, especially in Rome, enabled him to leave as considerable a mark on the city as any buried Caesar or Pope had done before his day. That influence was occasionally detrimental, but far more often beneficial.

When he inaugurated the Foro Mussolini (now the Foro Italico), north of the city, he was quite obviously anxious to emulate the Roman Caesars of bygone days; for it included a mammoth Olympic stadium accommodating 50,000 spectators, a smaller Marble Stadium (Stadio dei Marmi) with seats for 20,000, open and covered swimming-baths, tennis-courts, a hostel for visiting athletes and so on. All this architecture is rather pompous, but the sixty colossal marble statues of athletes surrounding the Stadio dei Marmi (hence its name) are frankly though unintentionally ridiculous, with their bulging muscles and hypertrophied limbs—surely expressive of the Duce's own exaggerated tastes? Italians do not in fact look like that!

The architect employed by Mussolini for the inception and development of his grandiose schemes was Marcello Piacentini (1881–1960), born in Rome. He was the son of Pio Piacentini (1846–1928), an architect who had been placed second in the great competition of 1885 for the monument to Vittorio Emanuele, won by Sacconi as already mentioned (p. 154). Marcello Piacentini became a teacher of town-planning in the School of Architecture at the university of Rome, and won several competitions, including that for the Triumphal Arch at Genoa (1923). He was therefore firmly established when Mussolini entrusted him with the important layout of the Foro Mussolini in 1928. Two years later came the rebuilding of the university of Rome, which was carried out in 1930–5 on a new site, as the Città Universitaria. The layout of the numerous buildings and the design of the Rettorato (Administrative Block) are by Piacentini himself; but he also directed the work of a number of other architects (named in the list on pp. 162–3) on the departmental buildings of the various faculties. The layout is pleasant enough, with paved walks under pergolas across gardens between the blocks of buildings, which are simple rather than impressive in design.

In 1937 Mussolini set Piacentini to work on a still larger enterprise, the enormous Esposizione Universale di Roma

(commonly called "E.U.R." for short), occupying a site
of about 1,000 acres, 5 miles south of the city. This
exhibition was planned to be opened in 1942, but the
outbreak of the Second World War prevented it. Its
layout is dignified and attractive enough, but most of the
buildings are simple or even commonplace rather than
distinguished. They include—somewhat surprisingly—an
austere domed church (SS. Pietro e Paolo) and a perfectly
hideous structure, the Palazzo della Civiltà Italiana, which
can be seen from 20 miles away. Six storeys high, it has a
range of nine arches on each storey of each front, without
a cornice or any other feature to break its monotony. It
suggests a gigantic columbarium, 227 feet high and 170
feet square on plan.

Piacentini's drastic clearance of the Borgo—the picturesque if shabby pair of streets leading from the Ponte
S. Angelo to Bernini's magnificent colonnaded Piazza di
S. Pietro—has been severely criticized. His new Via della
Conciliazione (1934–7) was his interpretation of a scheme
propounded centuries earlier, but his solution of the
problem is commonly regarded as vandalism. Something unpretentious was clearly desirable, and Piacentini
might have achieved it if only he had omitted the rows
of pompous columns lining the new street, which might
then have passed muster.

Mussolini was still in power when an architectural competition took place in 1938 for the new Central Railway
Station in Rome. It was won by a group of architects,
named on p. 162, who have since produced the largest
modern building in the city, and one of the finest railway
stations in the world.

Of other buildings erected in Italy during the fascist
period, and listed on pp. 162–3, little need be said here,

except that some of the new government buildings are very dull and undistinguished. The numerous new bridges across the Tiber in Rome can hardly be classified as works of architecture; but some mention must be made of the new towns established in the Campagna: at Littoria (now Latina, 1932); Sabaudia, near Nettuno (1934); Pontinia, near Terracina (1935); Guidonia (1935); and Aprilia (1937). The two last-named were very severely damaged in the Second World War. All are sensibly planned, with buildings of a generally simple character.

Mussolini's work in replanning Rome seems to me, as one who has known the city for more than fifty years, to be wholly admirable. From the beginning he continued schemes of slum clearance and street improvement begun by his predecessors. Then, always with one eye on his remoter predecessors, the Caesars, he commissioned Piacentini in 1931 to prepare a Piano Regolatore (Master Plan) which, while providing for the greatly increased motor traffic of a large city, should also pay respect to its many ancient monuments. Thus the much-needed new avenue, the Via dei Fori Imperiali, from the Piazza Venezia to the Colosseum, through the Archaeological Zone, is schemed to create the minimum of disturbance of important antiquities; while other relics of the past have been reverently cleared of accretions and framed in pleasant gardens. Above all the wonderful circuit of walls, gateways and towers—some twelve miles in length—enclosing the classical city has been revealed in its former grandeur. Taking his treatment of architecture in Rome as a whole we may feel grateful to Mussolini, whatever may have been his failings in other directions.

BUILDINGS OF THE FASCIST PERIOD
(1922–43)

1922	Florence. Cinema-Theatre Savoia	
		M. Piacentini
1923–32	Genoa. Triumphal Arch (competition)	,,
1925	Rome. Teatro Quirinetta	,,
1926	,, Albergo degli Ambiasciatori	,,
1927	,, Ippodromo di Villa Glori	,,
1928	Messina. Palazzo di Giustizia	,,
,,	Rome. Ministry of Air	R. Marino
,,	,, Ministry of Marine	G. Magni
1928 on	,, Foro Italico (sports centre), including Stadio Olimpico, Stadio dei Marmi, open and covered baths, hostel, etc. Piacentini & others	
1930–2	Florence. Municipal Stadium	P. L. Nervi
1930–4	,, Central Station (competition) Baroni, Berardi, Lusanna, Michelucci, Gamberini, Guarnieri	
1930–5	Rome. University, layout and Rettorato	
		Piacentini
	,, ,, Department of Letters and Philosophy	G. Rapisardi
	,, ,, Department of Law and Political Science	,,
	,, ,, Department of Hygiene and Surgery	A. Foschini
	,, ,, Department of Physics	P. Aschieri
	,, ,, Department of Geology, etc.	G. Michelucci
	,, ,, Department of Botany and Pharmacy	G. Capponi
	,, ,, Students' Hostel	G. Calza-Bini

PLATE XV

Rome: Central Railway Station (*Photo: Alinari*)

Rome: Olympic Stadium (*Photo: Alinari*)

PLATE XVI

Rome: Palazzetto dello Sport, exterior (*Photo by courtesy of the Cement and Concrete Association*)

Rome: Palazzetto dello Sport, interior (*Photo by courtesy of the Cement and Concrete Association*)

1930–5	Rome. University, Circolo del Littorio
	G. Minnucci
	„ „ Monumental entrance
	A. Foschini
1932–6	Naples. Central Post Office (competition)
	Vaccaro & Franzi
1933	Rome. Church of Cristo Rè Piacentini
„	„ Church of Madre di Dio C. Bazzani
1933–4	Venice. Multi-storey garage Official architects
1933–5	Bologna. School of Engineering G. Vaccaro
1934–7	Rome. Via della Conciliazione
	Piacentini & Spaccarelli
1936 on	Milan. Palazzo di Giustizia Piacentini
1937 on	Rome. Esposizione Universale ("E.U.R.")
	Planned for 1942; interrupted by war
	Piacentini & others
1938–50	„ Central Railway Station
	Calini, Castellazzi, Fadigati,
	Montuori, Pintanello, Vitellozzi
1938–56	„ Foreign Ministry (competition) —
	„ Ministry of War R. Marino

14

Architecture after Mussolini

1943 - 60

AFTER MUSSOLINI'S FALL from power in 1943, and before his sordid "liquidation" in 1945, the allied armies, British and American, fought through Italy from its southern tip to the Alps. Their slow but victorious advance—which reached the line Naples–Termoli in October 1943 and the line Pisa–Ravenna at the end of 1944—naturally involved heavy casualties among architectural monuments in many places; but some cities escaped with little or no damage, as is shown in the lists of buildings following my earlier chapters. Venice, Orvieto, Lecce, Perugia and Assisi survived intact. Rome suffered no more harm than a bomb on S. Lorenzo fuori and slight damage to the modern Città Universitaria. Many important buildings in Turin, Milan, Brescia, Vicenza, Bologna, Florence, Genoa, Rimini, Ravenna, Verona, Ancona, Naples, Messina, Catania and Palermo suffered severely. The famous Benedictine monastery of Montecassino was practically obliterated; but that at Subiaco remained almost intact.

In June 1946 Italy became a republic, and in the

following year signed a treaty with the Allies. Apart from the necessity to repair war damage (which, of course, included many buildings besides historical monuments) the country was still licking its wounds for the next few years. Poverty was widespread, and it is remarkable that architecture recovered so rapidly after the war years. Several projects initiated before the war by Mussolini and the fascist government were now brought to completion. In Rome, for example, the Central Railway Station (p. 163) was finished; the church of La Divina Sapienza was added to the Città Universitaria; and a stark new central post office was built near the E.U.R. (p. 163), for which the architects were the firm of Banfi, Belgiojoso, Peressutti & Rogers. The same firm, which has produced so many dignified buildings, is also responsible for an enormous skyscraper, the Torre Velasca, at Milan (1958). A recent critic described this curious structure, with its complete disavowal of Piacentini's simple architecture in the previous period (p. 159), as "baffling . . . and certainly provocative. . . . This is a tall office block in which the six top storeys project from the stem of the tower on concrete brackets, giving it the silhouette of a very Big Ben or an absurdly blown-up version of the bracketed top of the central tower of the Palazzo Sforzia [this should be the Castello Sforzesco] which commands the main axis of the city."[1] In Rome the new buildings of the Foreign Ministry adjoining the Foro Italico, on which work began in 1938, were opened in 1950. New bridges over the Tiber were the Ponte Flaminio (1951) and the Ponte Guglielmo Marconi (1955).

A branch of architecture in which contemporary

[1] Professor R. Gardner-Medwin, *R.I.B.A. Journal*, lxv, p. 410. Oct. 1958.

Italian architects excel is the design of apartment houses or residential flats, of all grades from *de luxe* to the artisan type. They are to be seen in many Italian cities, but especially in Rome, Milan and Naples. In Rome there are innumerable flats at very high rentals in the Parioli quarter (near the British School). They show great originality in design, ingenuity in planning, and a tendency to stark white walls and shutters: doubtless they contain every imaginable labour-saving gadget, for Italian electrical engineers are clever, and coal fires are unthinkable in most parts of the country. It would be invidious to attempt to list here the names of the chief architects who have specialized in this branch of design.

If one name stands out today as representative of contemporary Italian architecture in its most original form, it is that of Pier Luigi Nervi, who was born at Sondrio near Milan on 21st June 1891 and graduated in engineering at Bologna in 1913. He has already been mentioned here (p. 162) as designer of the Municipal Stadium at Florence (1930–2), holding 35,000 persons; and in the next decade he designed remarkable hangars for aircraft at Orvieto (1936) and Orbetello (1941). All these are works of structural engineering rather than of architecture as usually understood; and it was as an engineer, not as an architect, that he had graduated. He has shown an ability amounting to genius in his design of domes and other forms of roofing in reinforced concrete; has also devised a system of prefabricated units and movable shuttering for this form of construction; and in 1946 became Professor of Construction in the Architectural Faculty of the university of Rome. His later buildings include exhibition halls at Turin (1947–50); a salt warehouse at Tortona (1950), a tobacco factory at Bologna

(1950–2); the Gatti textile factory at Rome (1951); baths at Chianciano, including a hall with a wonderful domed roof (1950); the casino at the Lido di Roma (1950). He was either mainly or jointly responsible for the marvellous new railway station at Naples resulting from a competition won jointly with G. Vaccaro and M. Campanella in 1954; the Pirelli Building at Milan (1955–6); the Palazzetto dello Sport at Rome (1957), with a concrete dome 192 feet in diameter and accommodation for 5,000 persons; and the still larger Palazzo dello Sport (1959), also at Rome, on the E.U.R. site (cf. p. 160), another domed sports stadium, with a diameter of 330 feet and a seating capacity of 16,000. Both these buildings, designed for the Olympic Games of 1960, have vast fan-like roofs of *ferrocemento*; and a recent writer hardly exaggerates when he writes that the Palazzo dello Sport "has achieved in the 20th century what the Pantheon did in the 2nd century." Nervi was also joint architect of the U.N.E.S.C.O. building at Paris (1958).

He was awarded the Royal Gold Medal for Architecture of the R.I.B.A. for the year 1960—the highest honour in my profession.

FOR FURTHER READING

CHAPTER I

Dinsmoor, W. B., *The Architecture of Ancient Greece* (3rd ed.), 1950, Fyfe, D. T., *Hellenistic Architecture*, 1936, Plommer, H., *Ancient and Classical Architecture*, 1936, Randall-MacIver, D., *Italy before the Romans*, 1928, Randall-MacIver, D., *The Etruscans*, 1927, Randall-MacIver, D., *Greek Cities in Italy and Sicily*, 1931, Robertson, D. S., *Greek and Roman Architecture* (2nd ed.), 1943.

M

CHAPTER II

Plommer, H., *Ancient and Classical Architecture*, 1936, Robertson, D. S., *Greek and Roman Architecture* (2nd ed.), 1943, Anderson, W. J., *Architecture of Ancient Rome*, 1927, Middleton, J. H., *The Remains of Ancient Rome* (2 vols.), 1892, Rivoira, G. T., *Roman Architecture*, 1925, Vitruvius, *De Architectura* (Loeb Library, 2 vols.), 1931–4.

CHAPTER III

Hamilton, J. A., *Byzantine Architecture* (2nd ed.), 1956, Jackson, Sir T. G., *Byzantine and Romanesque Architecture*, 2 vols. (2nd ed.), 1920.

CHAPTER IV

Jackson, Sir T. G., *Byzantine and Romanesque Architecture*, 2 vols. (2nd ed.), 1920, Ricci, C., *Romanesque Architecture in Italy*, 1925, Rivoira, G. T., *Lombardic Architecture*, 2 vols. (2nd ed.), 1933.

CHAPTER V

Jackson, Sir T. G., *Gothic Architecture* (vol. II, Italy, etc.), 1915.

CHAPTERS VI, VII, VIII

Anderson, W. J., *Architecture of the Renaissance in Italy* (5th ed.), 1927, Jackson, Sir T. G., *The Renaissance of Roman Architerture* (vol. I, Italy), 1921–3.

CHAPTERS IX, X, XI

Briggs, M. S., *Baroque Architecture*, 1912, Ricci, C., *Baroque Architecture in Italy*, 1912, Wittkower, R., *Art and Architecture in Italy, 1600–1750*, 1958.

CHAPTER XIII

Pica, A., *Nuova Architettura Italiana*, 1936.

CHAPTER XIV

Pagani, C., **Architettura** *Italiana Oggi*, 1955.

Useful comment on architecture and contemporary social life in Italy, especially Rome, is provided in the *Journal of Montaigne's Travels in Italy, etc . . . in 1580 and 1581* (English translation, 1903); and in the *Diary of John Evelyn*, who visited Italy as a very observant and studious young man in 1644–5.

Index

176 INDEX

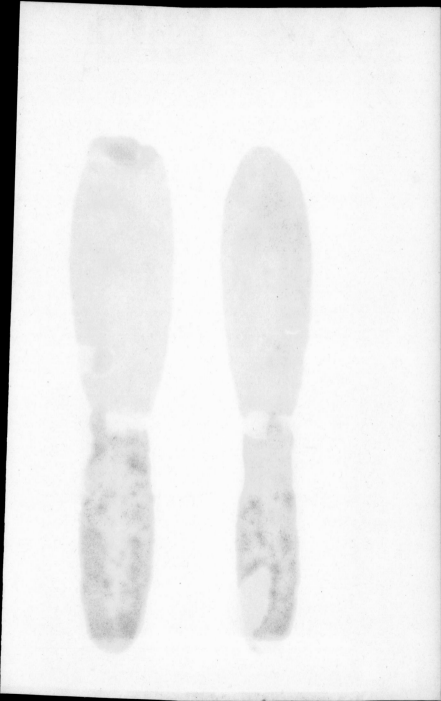